Kidding
AROUND THE
Gorge

D0048536

Written by Ruth Berkowitz and Lisa Kosglow
Book design by Gretchen Bayless and Audrey Moran

Printed in Hood River, OR by Columbia Gorge Press
ISBN: 978-0-692-44094-0
Cover photograph: Blaine Franger, www.blaineandbethany.com
Maps created by Mike Schrankel, Dennis Stilwell of Northwest Hiker, Hood River Valley Park and
Recreation District, US Forest Service and Northern Wasco County Park and Recreation.
Book Design: Gretchen Bayless and Audrey Moran
Please email us your suggestions or photographs for our 4th edtion
kiddingaroundthegorge@gmail.com.

Dedication

To the fantastic families and friends who make the Gorge an incredible place to play, live and kid around. Thank you for inspiring us to seize the day!

Acknowledgements

Kidding Around the Gorge would not have been possible without the assistance from our family and friends. Their wisdom, talent and input has helped us create the best edition of *Kidding* so far. Photographers have generously given us their photographs and parents and friends have answered our questions, providing us with ideas for new adventures.

An enormous appreciation and thank you to photographers Robin Dickinson, Blaine Franger and Paloma Ayala who gave us full access to their incredible photographs and spent time editing and preparing their images for this book. We also want to thank photographers Margot Angstrom, Jocelyn Akins, Nicholas Bielemeier, Clint Bogard, Andrew Bryden, Steven Datnoff, Ellen Dittebrandt, Nicole and Jeff Faaborg, the Fitzsimmons family, Peter Foley, Bethany Franger, Jim Greenleaf, Jeff Greenwood, Richard Hallman, Jurgen Hess, Darcy Hunter, Peter Marbach, Lora Melkonian, Jan Meyer, Melanie McCloskey, Maura Muhl, Ray Perkins, Maya and Tim Rayle, Scott Rumsey, Peter Rysavy, Kaori Stewart, and Brett VandenHeuvel.

Humongous appreciation to Gretchen Bayless for lending her love of the Gorge and design prowess to this third edition. Big thank yous to Monique Anderson-Pelletier and Kass Bergstrom for helping set the tone for the book, proofers and sounding boards Margot Angstrom, Scott Cook, Sue Davis, Lorri Epstein, Tonia Farman, Steve Gates, Jim Kosglow and Liz Whitmore. Thank you to Jody Barringer for the inspiration and teamwork on the first *Kidding* Book.

Ruth couldn't have written this book without her husband Tim, who held her hands through computer crises and her two children, Maya and Kai, who joined her on great adventures and taught her to see the Gorge through children's eyes.

Lisa specially thanks Jeff Greenwood for his love and support and for always carrying a GoPro or camera and Emilia for being patient and willing while mom tries out her parenting experiments.

Table of Contents

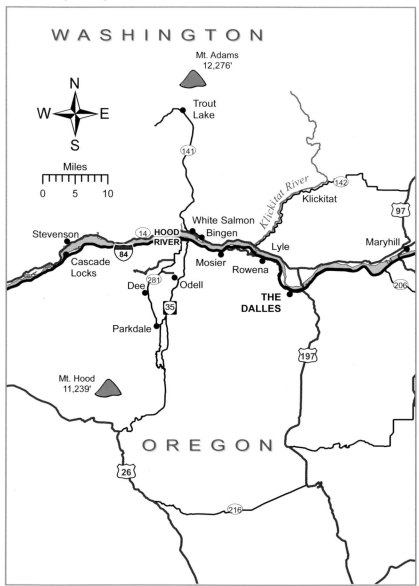

WASHINGTON

Mt. Adams
12,276'

N
W E
S

Miles
0   5   10

Trout
Lake

141

Klickitat River

142

97

Klickitat

White Salmon
Bingen

14 HOOD
RIVER

Stevenson

84

Cascade
Locks

Lyle

Maryhill

Mosier

281

Dee

Odell

35

Rowena

206

THE
DALLES

Parkdale

Mt. Hood
11,239'

197

OREGON

26

216

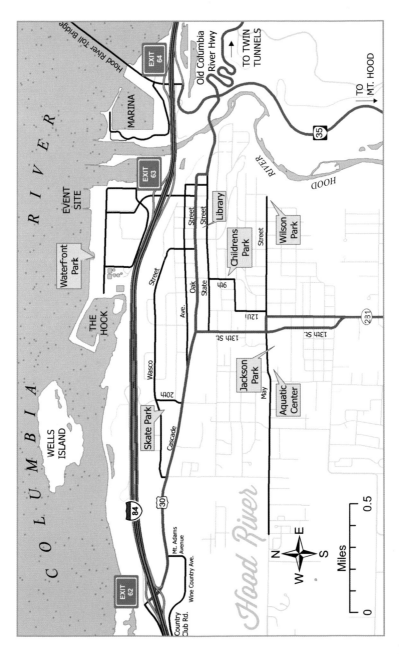

Introduction

We're thrilled you're holding the third edition of *Kidding Around the Gorge*. Our first two editions were good, but this one is fantastic. Not only is it in full color, but it also shows years of exploration and wisdom from many parents.

Since the second edition published in 2008, Ruth and her family sailed across the Pacific Ocean. When she returned three years later, her kids, Maya and Kai, grew into teenagers. Ruth continued to kid around, but she wanted to find an adventurous Mom with a young child who could bring fresh insight into the book. While hiking to see the petroglyphs, she met Lisa Kosglow, mom of a five year old, Olympic snowboarder, and founder of Let's Get Out, a jammed packed adventure camp based in the Gorge. We've become a great team! Together, we provide the inside scoop of what to do with your toddlers or teenagers.

Rain or shine, the Gorge is full of opportunities for fun and adventure - whether you want to hike, ski, bike, visit a museum, take a class, pick fruit or eat ice cream. It's all here. Not only is the Gorge a huge playground, but it's also a magical place to raise a family. As you explore the area, you'll see why kids together with their parents and grandparents are smiling - not to mention very busy kidding around in the fresh air.

We intentionally do not provide a detailed and exhaustive list of every possible place to explore. Instead, we describe some of the best kid-friendly places. When you're not sure what to do for the day or you have a few hours earmarked for exploration, open this book, pick an activity and get going! All activities listed are kid-tested. Places with a super smile next to them means that if you are only visiting for a short time, then these are the places you don't want to miss.

We have not received any endorsements. What follows are our opinions and ideas that we wanted to share with you. We are so thankful for all our friends and local photographers who contributed to this book. This is a community effort.

Thanks for reading and Happy Kidding! ~ *Lisa and Ruth*

How to Use This Book

This book divides into 18 Chapters ranging from playing at playgrounds, to hiking and biking to picking fruit and winter fun. Altogether, you'll find more than 200 different places to go or things to do with your child or someone else's child.

Most activities include a "Getting There" section. That's to make sure you don't drive in circles, like we have numerous times. We've tried to write the directions as straightforward as possible. To be consistent, all directions start from Hood River. To supplement the directions, we've included maps for you to use. We encourage you to pick up a more detailed map of the Gorge at one of the visitor centers in town or to consult Google Maps.

In Appendix B, the information is organized by location. That way, if you find yourself in The Dalles, Mosier, or any other town in the Gorge, you can look at Appendix B and get a bunch of ideas of where to go or what to do.

Smiley faces indicate the exceptional outings. Although everything listed in the book is worthwhile, the places with the smiley are the best of the best. If you have a limited time in the Gorge, make sure to go to the smileys.

Lastly, we want to warn you that there is some repetition because not everything fits in a square peg or a round hole. For example, Post Canyon is an ideal place to mountain bike and balance bike so you'll find it mentioned in a number of places. We've tried to minimize the repetition, but sometimes…well we don't want to repeat ourselves. Just use the book, keep it in your purse, backpack or car and have fun exploring the Gorge.

Key

Places you don't want to miss

Area

Distance

Level of difficulty:
1. Easy
2. Moderate
3. Difficult

Seasons open/best enjoyment:

❄ Winter

🌀 Spring

☀ Summer

✳ Fall

❋ Year round

🧭 **Directions for getting there**

Photo by Lisa Kosglow

CHAPTER 1

Monkeying
AROUND THE
Playground

Jipping at Westside

Photo by Brett Vandenheuvel

Gus getting tubed

When your kids turn your house into a playground, using the curtains as swings and the bed as a trampoline, it's time to head outside. Rest assured, we have many fun parks for children to let their wild energy gallop freely. Remember to bring sunscreen during the summer and hats in the winter.

- Cascade Locks Marine Park
- Children's Park
- Daubenspeck Park and Bingen Skatepark
- Hood River Waterfront Park
- Jackson Park
- Sorosis Park
- Tollbridge Park
- Wilson Park

Cascade Locks Marine Park

Area: Cascade Locks, OR

Located on the banks of the Columbia River with the historic locks and canal, the Cascade Locks Marine Park offers plenty of fun. Kids can climb on the boat themed play structure overlooking the water and then cross the bridge to Thunder Island and run around and explore the grassy area surrounded by trees. On the east side of the park, venture towards the boats in the marina and touch the stunning, larger-than-life bronze sculptures of Sacagawea and Merriweather Lewis' dog Seamus. The petite Historical Museum, bathrooms and picnic area are close by so you can make this an extended stop.

Getting There: From Hood River head west on I-84 to Exit 44, Cascade Locks. Drive west on Wa Na Pa Street. Look for the Sternweeler/ marina sign on the right side of the road, turn right just before the Eastwind Drive-In. (541) 374-8619 • www.portofcascadelocks.org

😊 Children's Park
📍 *Hood River, OR*

Built by the community of Hood River in just five days, the Children's Park is most popular for younger children. The wooden play structures include slides, tunnels, a large tic-tac-toe game, a sand area and oodles of places to explore.

Swinging at the park

Usually plenty of friendly parents are sitting on the benches or chatting away. Dribble the basketball in the covered court or run around for freeze tag in the large grassy area. Be warned that this park can be especially exposed to the hot summer sun so pack sun hats and check the slides on the playground—the metal can be scorching to touch. With the numerous structures and play areas, children can get lost. Public restrooms and water fountain are locked in the winter.

🧭 **Getting There:** From downtown, go west on Oak St. Make a left at 9th St., drive up the hill a few blocks and turn left on Hazel St. (541) 386-2383 • www.ci.hood-river.or.us

Daubenspeck Park and Bingen Skatepark
📍 *Bingen, WA*

This playground in Bingen (rhymes with "Engin") has colorful and challenging play structures that are well suited for five to seven year olds. Older kids can roll around at the newly built skate park. Visit any day and you'll see kids of all ages on skateboards, scooters, bikes and balance bikes. If you're lucky, you may also be skating with the local hot shots. For ball games, the park has a baseball backstop and a lighted basketball court. Bring your own food and enjoy the grassy picnic area complete with BBQ grills and tables. Public bathrooms have you covered for quick pit stops.

🧭 **Getting There:** Cross the Hood River Bridge to Washington, then turn right onto Hwy. 14. Drive one mile and make a left on Willow St. Look for the "City Park" sign. Bingen • (509) 493-2122

Hood River Waterfront Park
 Hood River, OR

The Waterfront Park symbolizes the hard work and creativity of our community. A small group of determined people fought vigilantly for decades to protect our prime waterfront area. Thanks to this special group and port authorities, we have a fabulous and imaginative park, as well as public and private office buildings and restaurants. Maneuver up the climbing wall, picnic in the sheltered area, build a sandcastle on the beach or play music on the giant xylophone. The paved paths are ideal for budding bikers and scooters. Many families swim in the Columbia and we like to as well, but take note that sadly sometimes our water quality is not up to par because of toxic pollution and unsafe bacteria levels. If you are concerned, please take a look at the Columbia Riverkeeper website, www.columbiariverkeeper.org for updated water quality reports or go to www.theswimguide.org and download the special app.

Getting There: From I-84, drive North from Exit 63 on 2nd Street. Turn left onto Portway and follow along until you reach the park on the river side of the street. www.hoodriverwaterfront.org

Busy day at the beach

Photo by Brett VandenHeuvel

Photo by Jeff Greenwood

Race you to the top!

Jackson Park
🅰 *Hood River, OR*

Located in the center of Hood River, Jackson Park has an outdoor stage, a play structure and a grassy hill for kids to run up and roll down. You'll appreciate the tall shady trees during the hot summer when families congregate for numerous events, including the Fourth of July picnic, evening concerts, and movies. Consider picnicking here after a swim at the community pool down the street. You can also play baseball at the well-manicured diamond. When it snows, the hills are ideal for sledding. Public restrooms.

🧭 **Getting There:** From downtown, go west on Oak St., south on 13th St. and turn right on May St. The park is at the corner of 13th and May Streets. (541) 386-2383 • www.ci.hood-river.or.us

😊 Sorosis Park
🅰 *The Dalles, OR*

This magnificent 15-acre park in The Dalles is worthwhile, not just for the view, but because there's plenty to do. Located on a high bluff overlooking the Columbia River, Sorosis Park is perhaps the biggest playground in the Gorge.

Photo by Lisa Kosglow

Running to the castle

You'll be pleasantly surprised with the castle-like wooden play structures, numerous swings, green grass, tall trees and picnic tables. You can play disc golf on the 18-hole golf course, toss horseshoes, or swing your racket. There's even a lovely rose garden. Public restrooms open all year round.

Getting There: From Hood River, drive 20 miles east on I-84 to Exit 83. Turn left onto 6th St., then right on Cherry Heights Rd., left on W. 9th St. and then right on Trevitt St. which becomes Scenic Dr. Wind up the curvy road to the park. (541) 296-9533 • www.nwprd.org

Toll Bridge Park
Parkdale, OR

Tucked away in Parkdale, this gem of a campground/park has play equipment, picnic tables with covered eating area and even a place to throw rocks and wade in the chilly Hood River. The water, the trees and the higher elevation keep this park cooler than many of the others which can be important on a hot summer day. The concrete sidewalk surrounding the play equipment is ideal for beginner bike riders. Kids can also pedal over to and around the campground and play by the river. Consider staying the night and sleeping under the stars – it's a great close-to-town camping option for a weekend "away."

Getting There: Take I-84 to Exit 64. Drive south on Hwy. 35 for 17 miles until you find signs for the park, near mile marker 84. Turn right on Toll Bridge Rd. (541) 352-5522 • www.co.hood-river.or.us

Wilson Park
🅐 *Hood River, OR*

This small neighborhood park scores high on the scale of places for kids to run around. The play equipment is geared for younger kids who can spend hours on the swings and the slides. The large lawn area is ideal for a picnic or running around plus there are some trees to seek refuge from the hot sun. No public restrooms.

🧭 Getting There:
Head west on Oak St., turn left onto 13th St. Drive up the hill and turn left onto May St. Continue to the end. 2nd and May St. (541) 386-2383 www.ci.hood-river.or.us

Photo by Jeff Greenwood

Wheee!

Other Playgrounds

In Hood River, try Oak Grove Park (Portland Dr. and Country Club Rd.). In White Salmon, play at Rhinegarten Park located at Lincoln and Main Streets. Stevenson has Rock Creek Park (at the Skamania Fairgrounds). When school is not in session, many of the playgrounds at the local schools are open to the public. Venture to Westside Elementary School (3685 Belmont Dr.), May St. Elementary School (10th and May Sts.) and Pine Grove School (2405 Eastside Rd.) in Hood River.

CHAPTER 2

Hikes WITH *Tikes*

Photo by Paloma Ayala • www.fotoisphoto.com

Follow Me

The Gorge is...gorgeous! Decorated with mountains, rivers, lakes and waterfalls, the Gorge is everyone's playground. When the wildflowers pop out in the early spring, take off your rain boots and lace up your hiking shoes. Some hikes are more challenging than others. Some lead to waterfalls, some have views, some are more protected from our strong winds, and others are paved and accessible for strollers. This Chapter divides into two sections: Paved/Dirt Trails and Waterfall and View Hikes. Enjoy!

- Historic Columbia River Highway
- Catherine Creek
- Indian Creek Trail
- Mosier Waterfront
- Sams Walker Trail
- Skamania Lodge Trails
- Tom McCall Nature Preserve
- Whoopdee Trail
- Beacon Rock and Rodney Falls

- Cape Horn
- Elowah Falls
- Falls Creek Falls
- Horsetail Falls
- Pacific Crest Trail
- Tamanawas Falls
- Wahkeena to Multnomah Falls

PAVED & DIRT TRAILS *Perfect* FOR STROLLERS

Many of the paved trails listed below are sections of the Old Columbia River Hwy., also known as Hwy. 30. Built by Sam Hill and Sam Lancaster between 1913 and 1922 when automobiles were smaller and a luxury, the Old Hwy. winds its way through our most scenic areas. Hill stated, "Good roads are more than my hobby, they are my passion." Some may ask "How in Sam Hill did they build this road?" We always wonder that when we make our way through the tunnel connecting Hood River

Just like Sam Hill

to Mosier. What an amazing feat to blast through the rock! In the 1950s, the wide Interstate-84 replaced the Old Highway. Today sections of the Old Highway have been re-paved and some parts are closed to vehicles, like the road from Hood River to Mosier and from Eagle Creek to Cascade Locks. These roads have become ideal places to hike, stroll and bike. On special days, the old Model-T's spark their engines, just like they did during the days of Sam Hill.

Historic Columbia River Highway
HCRH—Cascade Locks to Eagle Creek

📍 *Cascade Locks, OR*   ① *Easy*

🏃 *2.4 miles from Eagle Creek to Cascade locks*

☀ *Year round. Mostly protected from the wind.*

This 2.4 mile paved section of the Historic Columbia River Hwy. (HCRH) parallels I-84 from Eagle Creek to Cascade Locks and is stroller-friendly. You can start at either end of the trail. We prefer beginning at the Eagle Creek Fish Hatchery and strolling east to Cascade Locks. That way we investigate the fish in the beginning and enjoy ice cream at the end. The elevation gain is 65 feet and the road is fairly shady and lush. You pass Ruckels Creek and go through a tunnel that ends up on the north side of I-84. Here, play with your echo—it usually responds. Most of the trail avoids the busy freeway. Return on the same road or have a friend pick you up in Cascade Locks.

🧭 **Getting There:** Take I-84 west to Bonneville Dam Exit 40 and then double back east on the freeway one mile to the Eagle Creek Exit. The Old Highway trail starts to the right of the freeway.
(800) 551-6949 • www.oregonstateparks.org

Photo by Andrew Bryden

What's up...

😀 HCRH—Mark O. Hatfield Trailhead-Hood River to Mosier

📍 *Between Hood River and Mosier, OR*

② *Moderate*

🏃 *4.6 miles one way from Hood River to Mosier*

☀ *Year round. Not protected from the wind.*

Hood River to Mosier is the most popular paved section of the Historic Columbia River Highway (HCRH) attracting bikers, strollers, rollerbladers, bird watchers and lots of families. It's a perfect place for parents to get some exercise while their kids nap in the stroller. During the weekend, be careful of the bikers whizzing down the hill. On the rare occasions when we have snow down low, it's really exciting to ski on the trail and see the ice formations in the tunnels. When you're in the tunnels, look for the etching on the wall by people stranded for 12 days in a snow storm in November 1921. What would you do if you were stranded?

Getting There: Take Exit 64 and drive south on Hwy. 35. Turn left at the 4-way stop. Follow Old Columbia Hwy. to the parking lot at the end. (800) 551-6949 • www.oregonstateparks.org

HCRH—Starvation Creek to Viento

- **Approximately 5 miles west of Hood River**
- **Easy**   **2 miles**
- **All seasons**

This resurrected section of the Historic Columbia River Highway (HCRH) is short, mostly shady and closed to automobiles, though the first part parallels the busy Interstate. Kids can safely meander the one-mile stretch. You can park at either Starvation Creek or Viento. Logistically, if you're coming from Hood River, you might want to park at Viento because it's a few miles closer than driving to the Starvation Creek Exit. Pack a picnic to enjoy when you reach Starvation Creek Falls.

What an amazing place

Photo by Ellen Dittebrandt

Getting There: Take I-84 west from Hood River to Exit 56. Turn left under the freeway to Viento State Park. (800) 551-6949 www.oregonstateparks.org

Catherine Creek

Ⓐ Between Bingen and Lyle, WA
① ② Easy to moderate
🏃 Varies   ❄ All seasons

Come during the springtime and you'll be rewarded with spectacular wildflowers and sensational views of the Columbia River and Mt. Hood. The one mile paved trail starts with a gentle downhill walk through open grassy areas and ponds. Carefully maneuver your way down the steep hill to get closer to the waterfall. Another option is to hike the dirt road to the natural arches which you can access on the north side of the road. Enter the gate and take the first path on the right. This trail follows the creek and depending on the water level, traversing may be tricky. You'll pass an old abandoned homestead on your way to the top of the rock arch. Beware of poison oak and ticks. During the spring, we often look for tadpoles at the pond/water hole located at the top of the hill straight up from the parking lot.

🧭 **Getting There:** Cross the Hood River Bridge and turn right on Hwy. 14. Drive 4.6 miles, turn left onto Old Hwy. 8/ County Road 1230 (between mile markers 70 and 71). Pass Rowland Lake and follow the road 1.4 miles to the Catherine Creek parking lot on the north side of the road. www.fs.fed.us

Goin' on an egg hunt

Indian Creek Trail

Hood River, OR

Easy to moderate

Varies   **All seasons**

The Indian Creek Trail might eventually connect, but today it divides into four segments. We like to escape to the trail when we're pressed for time or in need of a quick commune with nature. Depending on where you're located, you can access the trail on Hazel Street, 12th Street, the Columbia Gorge Community College, the Hood River Valley High School, Fairview Drive, and on Barrett Road about a mile west of Windmaster corner. The trail has bridges to cross, and a rushing creek for stick throwing and wading. In the late summer, feast on the blackberries scattered along the

trail. We are thankful to have this meandering path spread around our town. Hopefully in the future, we'll be able to walk or bike it from one end to the next.

Photo by Robin Dickenson

Racing down the trail

Indian Creek Trail, near Columbia Gorge Community College

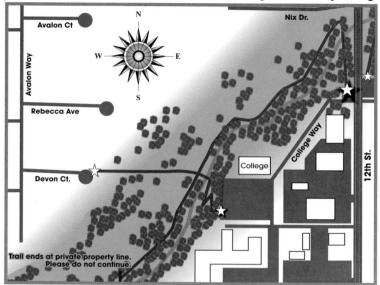

Indian Creek Trail, near Hood River Valley High School

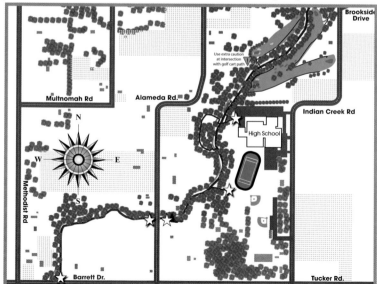

Fairview Drive, near Westside Elementary

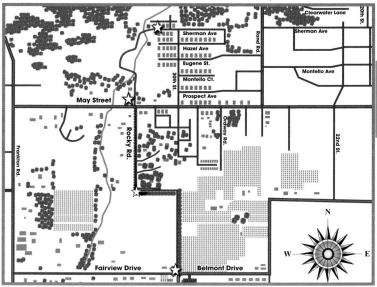

Hazel Street to 12th Street

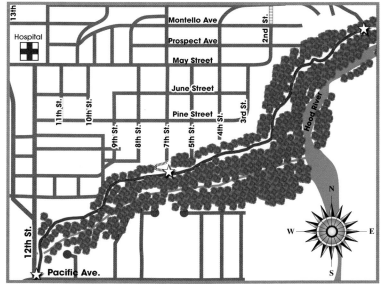

25

Leaves of three, let them be!

Mosier Waterfront

- 🅐 *Mosier, OR*
- ① *Easy*
- 🏃 *Varies*
- ❄️ *Year round, but can be crowded during the summer if it's windy*

Poison Oak

"Leaves of three, let it be." Poison Oak grows prolifically in the Gorge and comes in different colors and forms. The leaves can be green, red or both. They can be shiny or dull. They can be spade shaped or more like an oak leaf. The poison spreads through a resin called urushiol which gets absorbed in your skin and then surfaces as a red rash. If you get the rash, Margaret from Mother's Marketplace taught us to slice a potato and place the potato on top of the infected area. The potato dries your skin and relieves most of the itching. Other's recommend an oatmeal bath and cool water. Tecnu or rubbing alcohol helps for some, especially if applied shortly after contact. Remember not to scratch—it gets worse.

Looking for a short walkabout in Mosier and don't mind the hum of the highway? Venture to Rock Creek trailhead for several options. One place is to start at the southeast corner of the parking area and follow the trail through oak and blackberries to the wetland. Be aware of the train tracks and keep a close eye on your darting young ones. Here there are two different overlooks where you can look for soaring eagles. However, instead of live birds, we found numerous dead bird carcasses. But don't squeal—they're fascinating for the budding scientist. You can continue east on the trail until it wraps around and pops out on the beach along the Columbia River. Walk west along the beach back to the parking area. For quicker access to the beach, head north of the parking area and follow the trail. This portion of the trail is stroller accessible with benches along the path and plenty of places to throw rocks.

Getting There: Take I-84 east from Hood River to Mosier Exit 69. Turn right and take the first left, leading you under the freeway to Rock Creek Rd. Plenty of parking as long as it isn't windy.

Sams Walker Trail

 Stevenson, WA **Easy**
 1.1 miles **Year round**

Looking for a relaxing hike that's stroller friendly and toddlers can safely run ahead while you chat with your friend. This trail might be perfect. The loop starts with an open meadow where both the Sams and Walker families' horses and cows grazed. These two families homesteaded here from 1903 to 1969. Your hike takes you towards the river with lots of blackberry bushes. As you meander west, past the cottonwoods and the tall willows, you enter a secluded trail surrounded by old oak and cedar trees. Beware of mosquitoes. Peruse the interpretive signs along the way. Back at the meadow with the tall grass and wildflowers, you'll find a stellar view of the top of Beacon Rock.

Getting There: Head west on I-84 for 18.6 miles to Exit 44. Cross The Bridge of the Gods and continue 8.9 miles west on Hwy. 14 until the second Skamania Landing Road located at mile 33. The road is a loop. Don't take the first one at the east end. Cross the railroad tracks and drive for ¼ mile to the parking lot.

Skamania Lodge Trails

Stevenson, WA   **Easy**
Varies   **Year round**

Skamania Lodge has three trails that weave in and around the golf course. All are short and partially paved: the Creek Loop (1.5 miles), the Lake Loop (1.75 miles), and the Gorge Loop (1.0 miles). Pop into the hotel and grab a map. We like to walk the Lake Loop which has a view of the river and restrooms mid-way. Look for frogs in the pond, but watch out for golf balls along the way. If you come on a Friday, we highly recommend bringing a huge appetite and staying for their famous all-you-can-eat seafood buffet. Did anyone say oysters? Skamania Lodge also has a family golf program where kids can learn to play and zoom around in the golf carts. Children 60 pounds and heavier can fly through the trees in their super zippy ziplines.

Photo by Paloma Ayala • www.fotoisphoto.com

Laughing with Dad!

Getting There: Drive I-84 west from Hood River to Cascade Locks Exit 44. Cross the Bridge and turn right on Hwy. 14. Just before downtown Stevenson, you'll see signs to the Lodge. (800) 221-7117 • www.skamania.com

Tom McCall Nature Preserve

Between Mosier and The Dalles, OR

Easy to Difficult

Plateau trail is 1 mile; McCall Point trail is 2 miles

McCall Point is best in winter and spring; Plateau trail is open May-Oct

Named after Oregon Governor Thomas Lawson McCall (1967-1975), this hike is exceptional in the spring when the wildflowers decorate the mountain. Committed to preserving the environment, the Governor encouraged people to visit Oregon, but discouraged them from staying. You have two options for a hike: the Plateau Trail or the steeper two mile McCall Point trail. The later begins at the south side of the turnaround, gains 1,000 feet of elevation, has a few cliffy areas and takes you up to a stellar view of Mt. Hood and Mt. Adams. Although challenging for small legs, the view at the top and the flowers along the way are worth the effort. The easier Plateau Trail begins at the interpretive sign by the parking lot. This trail parallels the Rowena Dell ravine and leads to a large pond surrounded by oak trees and poison oak. Keep an eagle eye on your children especially near the ravine, which is a sheer cliff. In the spring, look for tadpoles and frogs. The non-profit Nature Conservancy owns the preserve and prohibits dogs, camping and picking flowers.

Getting There: Drive 5 miles east on I-84 to Mosier Exit 69. Turn left for 6 miles on Hwy 30 and you'll see the parking lot. (503) 230-1221 • www.nature.org

Blustery bluffs

Photo by Paloma Ayala • www.fotoisphoto.com

Whoop Dee Trail Systems

Hood River, OR   **Moderate**
Varies   **All seasons**

Thanks to SDS Lumber Company, these hilly trails on Hood River Mountain are open to the public. The area is extremely popular for mountain bikes, but it's also a fun place to hike. We like the ridge trail or tower trail as it has stunning views of the Hood River Valley and Mt. Hood. The trail takes you on a gentle hike up to the ridge where you can picnic with a view and then head back down the same path. This is the best option for jogging strollers. If your kids want more, after you reach the ridge, turn right on the path and take the narrow trail to the sensational viewpoint where it's possible to see all three mountains, Adams, Mt. St. Helens and Rainier. You can turn back or continue through the recently logged section down to the main road and make a loop. You'll have to walk back on the gravel road for one mile but it's a fun adventure. Bring a jacket because the ridge is exposed to wind. Watch for the yellow balsamroot wildflowers in the spring—they're all over and exquisite!

Getting There: From I-84 take Exit 64 and drive south on Hwy. 35 for 3 miles to Whiskey Creek Rd. (mile marker 100). Make a left on Eastside Rd. then an immediate right onto Old Dalles Road. This road turns into gravel. Once it does, drive 1.5 more miles until you see the gate on the right side of the road. Park on the left but watch out for the ditch. (509) 493-2155 • www.sdslumber.com

Photo by Peter Rysavy

Lea looking at Desert Paintbrush

Keep 'em Moving!

You've packed a lunch, water, snacks, extra clothes, diapers, sunscreen, hats, backpacks, camera, the dog, half the house and you reach the trail-head, eager to begin, except your child goes on strike. We've all been there! Here are some ideas for encouraging and motivating kids to get outside without shamelessly bribing them with screen time or sweets?

• **Look for fairies.** Do you know that fairies or elves might be living under the ferns, tucked into the crotches of trees or sleeping in hollowed out trunks? As you walk or pedal, ask your kids to look for treasures for the fairies. Small hemlock cones, smooth stones, soft feathers, pieces of driftwood, you get the idea. When you stop for lunch, build a fairy house out of any of the available materials and decorate it with new found treasures. To keep those little legs moving on the trail, team with your kids in telling a story or creating a song. Your engagement increases the fun factor!

• **Tell stories.** The trail is a perfect place to tap into everyone's creativity. Ask your child for a subject or prompt one. Consider your child's favorite storybook character or animal. Make sure to include your child or her name in the story (ex. a cat, ninja, train named after your child.) As you tell the story, ask for input, "what happens next?" "Where did they go?" "What did they do there?" "What did they eat?" Often kids will take over as the narrator and soon you'll be hiking along listening to their story without giving any input or hearing any "Are we there yet?" complaints.

• **Sticks can be safe.** Kids love sticks, but often parents fear them. Yes, they can be dangerous and kids can poke each other's eyes out. However, we've found on our hikes, ways to embrace the stick and keep it safe. Giving kids a few rules helps: we tell them they can pick up sticks, collect them, but never use them to hit or strike another person. By allowing your child to choose a walking stick or an exploration stick, she might enjoy the hike more as she uses her stick to poke holes, stir mud puddles or even draw pictures. No eyes go missing.

Kids love sticks

Photo by Blaine Franger
www.blaineandbethany.com

31

Waterfall and View Hikes

😊 Beacon Rock / Rodney Falls (Pool of Winds)

🔴 **N. Bonneville, WA**

② **Moderate with some handholding spots**

🏃 **Beacon Rock is 1.5 miles round-trip, Pool of Winds is 2.5 miles round-trip**

☀️ **Year round. Protected from wind (except at the top of the rock).**

Hike up the towering 848-foot Beacon Rock, named by explorers William Clark and Meriwether Lewis. In 1915, Henry Biddle bought the rock for one dollar and spent the next 15 years building the steep trail and equipping it handrails and bridges. It's a steep one mile, 52 switchback climb to the top and only advised for older kids or children who will obediently hold an adult's hand. At the summit, you'll be rewarded with a panoramic view of the Gorge. After this accomplishment, every time you drive pass Beacon Rock, smile and tell yourselves, "We climbed that monolith!" You would have wanted to be up here on the top 15,000 years ago when the ice and floods carved the Gorge because this is one of the few places, where you would have been safe.

The Pool of Winds/Rodney Falls hike takes you to the top of the three-tiered waterfall where you can physically feel the power of the falls as it bursts from the cliff. Begin at the campground for Beacon Rock State Park and take the

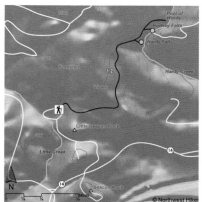

Safe from the floods

Hamilton Mountain Trailhead. First you walk through a steep path in the forest to Hardy Creek with a great view of the thundering falls. Follow the signs to Pool of the Winds. It's a perfect hike and the campground has restrooms and swings.

Getting There: From Hood River, drive I-84 west 16 miles to Cascade Locks Exit 44 and cross the Bridge of the Gods. Turn left on Hwy. 14. for about 7 miles until you see Beacon Rock Parking Lot. For Pool of Winds, follow the signs to the campground, which is equipped with picnic tables, swings, restrooms and running water. Beacon Rock State Park. (509) 427-8265 • www.parks.wa.gov

Cape Horn Trail (View Trail)

Area: Skamania County, WA
Moderate to difficult with lots of handholding spots
Nancy Russell Overlook 2.5 miles, full loop is 7.7 miles
Best in Spring and Fall.

This big kid hike can be a long 7.7 mile loop or a much shorter one to various viewpoints. For little ones, we suggest hiking 2.5 miles up to the Nancy Russell Overlook, named after one of the founders of Friends of the Gorge, who came here in the early 1980's when the area was slated to become a 16-lot private subdivision. Russell fought for 20-years to protect Cape Horn and its sweeping views. Thanks to her efforts, it's now a great place to explore.

Be warned that the steep cliffs at the overlooks are scary and require hand holding. The first overlook, Pioneer Point, is about 1 ¼ miles up the path. If you decide to continue on, the trail flattens and veers away from the river and takes you along an old wagon road. Eventually you'll reach the Russell Overlook (dedicated August 2011), with its expansive views. This makes for a great lunch spot. The lower part of the loop is closed from February 1 to July 15 to protect the nesting peregrine falcons. Please obey this closure; fines can be as high as $5000.

Getting There: Drive to Cascade Locks, cross the Bridge of the Gods, drive west on Hwy. 14 until milepost 26.5. Turn right at Salmon Creek Falls road. Public restrooms. www.capehorntrail.org

Photo by Margot Angstrom

That was quick!

Elowah Falls

📍 **Waterfall Alley, OR**
① **Easy**
🏃 **1.4 miles**
☀❄ **Spring to Fall**

This great beginning waterfall hike is short, not too steep (elevation gain of 280 feet) and rewarding. It's also one of the closest to Portland hikes we have in our book, so this may be a good option for families coming from the west. Park at the John B. Yeon Trailhead and walk about half a mile. Always stay left. Continue for another mile on a gentle ascent and then you'll find short switchbacks down to the base of Elowah Falls. The 290 foot waterfall plunges from an impressive amphitheater. For more adventure on your way back from the falls, head right at the junction and take the Upper McCord Creek Falls Hike. About a quarter mile up the steep switchbacks, you'll find box car boulders and remnants of the old flume pipe built around 1890 to transport water. We do not recommend taking your young kids all the way up the trail because of steep and scary spots where the trail cuts into the cliff. If you go up there, hold extremely tight to your little one. The view of the Gorge is stunning and the falls at Upper McCord Creek incredibly photogenic.

🧭 **Getting There:** From Hood River, head east on I-84 until Exit 37, Warrendale. Drive .3 miles, turn left under the bridge, left onto Frontage Rd. for .3 miles until the Parking Lot. From Portland, take Exit 35, Ainsworth, turn left at the stop sign, then immediately turn right on Frontage Rd. for 2.1 miles to the parking lot.

😀 Falls Creek Falls Trail

📍 **Carson, WA**   ② **Moderate**
🏃 **3.4 miles**   ☀❄ **Spring to Fall**

When you hike in this lush area, it feels like the trolls and fairies are also in the dense forest of fir and cedar trees. The trail gradually climbs 1.7 miles uphill winding through the ancient trees. You'll find plenty of logs to practice the balance beam and lots of big trees for hide and seek games. A snack overlooking the river will keep you fueled and energized. You'll cross two suspension bridges before reaching the misty base of the three-tiered 250-foot waterfall. Beware this is also a mountain bike trail, though a pretty challenging one for young kids.

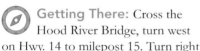
The Richmond boys love an adventure

Photo by Lisa Kosglow

Getting There: Cross the Hood River Bridge, turn west on Hwy. 14 to milepost 15. Turn right on Wind River Hwy. 30. Follow Mt. St. Helens signs for 15 miles. Turn right onto FR. 3062 for 2 miles until Road 57. Continue 1/4 mile to the trailhead.

Horsetail and Ponytail Falls
Waterfall Alley, OR
Difficult with some handholding spots
2.7 mile loop   Year round. Protected from wind.

Located in the most scenic area of the Old Columbia Highway (which we've named "Waterfall Alley"), the Horsetail Falls hike takes you physically behind Ponytail waterfall. Listening and watching the water stream down like thunder is awesome. The hike starts just to the east of Horsetail Falls. Your first .4 miles is a steep climb. At Ponytail Falls, you can turn around and go back to the car or continue on the lush green trail, making your way to the top of Oneonta Falls. There's a classic footbridge that crosses the river above Oneonta Falls. Continue down the trail and you'll end up less than half a mile from your car. If your kids are tired, have someone retrieve the car while you throw rocks into the river at the beginning of the Oneonta trail.

Getting There: Drive I-84 to Ainsworth Park Exit 35. From there continue west on the Old Hwy. for 1.5 miles to the Horsetail Falls parking lot. (541) 386-2333 • www.fs.fed.us

Pacific Crest Trail

① Cascade Locks (but possible from Mexico to Canada)
② Moderate
🏃 4.2 miles round trip   ☀ Year round

Lauded for being one of the finest trails in the country, this section of the PCT begins near the parking lot near the Bridge of the Gods in Cascade Locks. There is a gradual uphill for the first mile, but keep the little feet moving as the path flattens out. High on the cool factor, you can keep walking south all the way to Mexico—otherwise hike a little more than 2 miles to Dry Creek Falls, a 75-foot waterfall. The trail itself is 2,663 miles from the US border with Mexico all the way to Canada. It takes the average hiker about five months to traverse the 26 National Forests, 7 National Parks, 5 state parks and 3 national monuments. In your spare time, pick up a copy of Wild, written by Portland author Cheryl Strayed. This "how not to hike the PCT" book documents Strayed's experience on the trail. You can also watch the movie *Wild* starring Reese Witherspoon. Parts of the movie were filmed right here in Cascade Locks.

Getting There: From Hood River, take I-84 to Exit 44. Drive through Cascade Locks to the west side and turn left on the access road to the Bridge of the Gods. The trailhead parking lot is marked by an entrance sign on the right.

Tamanawas Falls

Mt. Hood, OR

Moderate to Easy with a little handholding

3.8 miles round-trip

Summer and fall. Protected from wind.

When it's hot in Hood River, head up Hwy. 35 to Mt. Hood. This mostly shady hike meanders over log bridges, through old growth trees, and along the streaming creek where you expect to end up at grandmother's house, but instead, find a waterfall. The Native Americans felt this, too, since Tamanawas means a friendly guardian spirit. The beginning of the trail has some steep parts where you won't want to lose sight of your children. Follow the Cold Spring Creek bed and the gradual 400-foot elevation gain brings you across boulders and then to the waterfall. You can walk close to the 100-foot falls, but beware, as it is always wet and slippery near waterfalls.

Getting There: Take I-84 to Exit 64 and drive 30 miles south on Hwy. 35. At milepost 72, drive .2 miles and park at the Sherwood Campground parking lot. The trailhead is on the right, close to the river.
(541) 352-6002 • www.fs.fed.us

Photo by Jocelyn Akins

Behind the falls

On the way to Wahclella

Wahclella Falls

- Waterfall Alley, OR
- **Easy**
- **2 miles round-trip**
- **Year round.**

This two-mile hike is a perfect first waterfall hike because it is short and relatively easy. The trail starts out wide with Tanner Creek on the right. As you walk into the canyon, the path becomes narrower and the maiden hair ferns carpet the hillside. You'll pass Munra Falls, a small waterfall on the way and then end up at the more impressive Wahclella Falls. If you look up to the top of Wahclella Falls, you can see East Fork Falls. On your return, take the path, across the bridge, for a short loop back to the main trail. You'll cross the creek and see a little cave that's fun to explore. During the spring, wildflowers scatter along the trail. When it's warm, splash around the creek near the waterfall. Although its just two miles, it often takes us hours to complete.

Getting There: Take I-84 to Bonneville Dam Exit 40. Go left away from the dam and cross under the freeway. Follow the sign for Wahclella Falls. (541) 386-2333 • www.fs.fed.us

Wahkeena to Multnomah Falls

🅰️ Waterfall Alley, OR

②③ Moderate to Difficult

🚶 4.8 miles round-trip   ✳️ Year round

This is one of our favorite hikes because it takes you to eight named waterfalls. Beware, the trail is challenging and a bit long (5 miles), but ice cream awaits at Multnomah Falls' Lodge. The first two miles are steep switchbacks. Follow Larch Mt. trail signs then turn left at Multnomah Creek and follow signs for Wahkeena trail 420. Continue for a little more than half a mile and the trail flattens out. The lush scenery makes you feel close to Frodo's home in The Hobbit. You'll pass seven waterfalls and end up at the top of the grand Multnomah Falls. That's when the trail can get pretty crowded. It's magnificent to peer down Oregon's largest waterfall. At the Lodge, we usually have someone walk the half mile back to the Wahkeena Falls parking lot to retrieve the car while we savor the soft serve ice cream and look at exhibits.

Getting There: Take I-84 west for 28 miles to Ainsworth Park Exit. 35. Continue west on the Old Hwy. to the Wahkeena Falls Picnic Trail. (541) 386-2333 • www.fs.fed.us

Eager to go

Parking Permits

Many trails in Oregon and Washington require a parking pass. You need a PhD to figure out what pass to buy. Here are the cliff notes:

• Northwest Forest Pass ($5/day; $30/year) includes parks in Oregon like Bonneville, Bridge of the Gods, Cloud Cap, Eagle Creek, Wahclella Falls, Wyeth, Tamanawas, etc. Trailheads in Washington like Dog Mt., Sams-Walker, Falls Creek Falls and other US Forest Service lands. U.S. Forest Service, (800) 270-7504, www.naturenw.org or www.fs.fed.us

• Oregon State Parks ($5/day; $25/year) includes Ainsworth State Park, Historic Columbia River Highway State Trail, Mayer State Park (Rowena), Memaloose State Park, Viento State Park, Deschutes State Recreation Area and other OR State Parks. (800) 452-2027, www.oregonstateparks.org

• Washington State Parks Discover Pass ($10/day; $30/year) includes Beacon Rock State Park, Horsethief Butte, Columbia Hills State Park, Doug's Beach, and other WA State Parks. (866) 320-9933, www.parks.wa.gov

• Washington and Oregon Recreation Pass: $100/year; this makes economic sense if you're planning on visiting the federal parks like Crater Lake, Fort Clatsop and Mt. Rainier. Otherwise, if you're staying in the Gorge, the Oregon, Northwest Forest and Washington, Discover Passes will suffice. (800) 270-7504, www.naturenw.org

• Sno-Park permits: Both Oregon and Washington require a Sno-Park permit from Nov. 1 to April 30th (each state issues its own permit). In Oregon, permits cost $25 annually; $4 daily (although some agents charge an extra fee). California and Idaho Sno-Park permits are valid in Oregon. Places requiring a permit include Mt. Hood Meadows, Cooper Spur, Government Camp, Ski Bowl, Trillium, and Little John. In Washington, permits are $40 annually and $20 daily (agents charge a $2 fee, but "daily" means three consecutive days) Other state permits are not recognized in Washington. Places requiring a permit include Ape Cave and some surrounding areas of Mt. St Helens as well as Snow King and some Trout Lake area trailheads.

Tips for Hiking with Kids

• Use "kid-speak" when preparing for a hike. Instead, of the daunting "let's go hike three miles," try "want to look for tadpoles?"; "ready to press flowers?" or "let's make tree rubbings."

• Bring special snacks, plenty of water, extra clothes, and sunscreen.

• Give your child her own backpack and water bottle.

• Try hiking with a GPS and looking for geocache hidden treasures. For more information see www.geocaching.com

• Play hide-and-seek along the trail.

• Remember, it's about the journey, not the destination. If you don't reach the waterfall, that's ok. Be a naturalist and examine the ferns, the slugs, the wildflowers and whatever else you encounter.

• Have your hiker document her trip with a camera or a notebook like Charles Darwin and Meriwether Lewis.

• Whistles. A good safety tool, whistles give children louder voices and may help in an emergency. Teach your kids when to blow them so they don't annoy other hikers.

CHAPTER 3

Bikin'
THE *Gorge*

We have premier biking here in the Gorge with miles of quiet country roads to explore. Whether you pedal through mud puddles or ride all the way up to the Mosier Twin Tunnels, either makes a perfect outing. This chapter divides into three sections: road biking, mountain biking and balance bikes.

- Historic Columbia River Highway

- Maryhilll Loop Road

- North Bonneville

- The Dalles Riverfront

- Eight Mile

- Knebal Springs Trail and Bottle Prairie

- Klickitat Rail Trail

- Post Canyon

- Ski Bowl

- Syncline

- White Salmon Bike Park

- Fort Cascades

- Hood River Waterfront

- Indian Creek

- Trillium Lake

Road Biking

HCRH—Eagle Creek to Cascade Locks

Cascade Locks, OR

Easy

2.4 miles from Eagle Creek to Cascade Locks

Year round. Mostly protected from the wind.

This 2.4 mile paved section of the Historic Columbia River Highway (HCRH) is also separate from cars and for the most part away from the highway noise. This section parallels I-84 from Eagle Creek to Cascade Locks. Although you can start at either end of the trail, we prefer parking at the Eagle Creek Fish Hatchery and biking east to Cascade Locks. The trail gradually climbs from the Eagle Creek Trailhead to just past Ruckels Creek. Kids can zoom down the hill into a tunnel that ends up on the north side of I-84. When you reach the Bridge of the Gods and Cascade Locks, bike east on Wa-Na-Pa St. less than a half mile to cool off with your choice of soft serve at the East Wind Drive In on WaNaPa Street. Return on the same road or have a friend pick you up.

Getting There: Take I-84 west to Bonneville Dam Exit 40 and then double back on the freeway for one mile until the Eagle Creek exit. The Old Highway trail starts to the right of the freeway. (800) 551-6949 • www.oregonstateparks.org

A little more of a climb

Photo by Jeff Greenwood

HCRH—Mark O. Hatfield Trailhead-Hood River to Mosier

Between Hood River and Mosier, OR   **Moderate**

4.6 miles one way from Hood River to Mosier

Year round. Not protected from the wind.

This section of the Historic Columbia River Highway (HCRH) is closed to cars and an ideal place to bike with your kids. It's challenging because the beginning is a gradual climb up to the twin tunnels. You'll pass a small trickling waterfall, fields of wildflowers (in the spring), blackberries in the summer and get great views of the Gorge. The trail can be busy with bikers zipping by. We love riding our bikes all the way to downtown Mosier for ice cream at the Route 30 Roadside Café. Sometimes one parent will ride home and bring the car, but if your kids have strong legs, you can do the whole trip. The trailhead in Hood River has restrooms and an informative Visitor's Center.

Getting There: Take I-84 to Exit 64. Go south to the four-way stop sign. Turn left on Old Columbia Hwy. Rd. and drive up the curvy road until you reach the Mark O. Hatfield State Park. (800) 551-6949 • www.oregonstateparks.org

Photo by Peter Foley

Maryhill Loop Road

Maryhill, WA   **Moderate/Difficult**
2.2 miles one-way
Year round. Exposed, not protected from wind

This paved road closed to cars is famous worldwide amongst skateboarders, street lugers and bikers for its hairpin corners and smooth asphalt. Every summer there's a speed competition where some competitors top 55 mph. The young slower bike rider can also enjoy the challenging curvy road. The path is perfectly paved for the first 2.2 miles, but the remaining half mile has not been repaved since it was built in 1913 by Sam Hill to help transport goods from Goldendale to the Columbia River. It is possible to continue up to Hwy. 97 and bike all the way to Goldendale, but you probably want to turn around and whiz down the hill. You'll have clear views of all the numerous wind turbines and your heart will beat fast when you watch your little one fly down the hill. At the entrance, look for tasty blackberry bushes and a creek to splash around. To expand your ride, bike 1.6 miles from the entrance of Maryhill Loop Road to Stonehenge. You will have to ride ¼ mile on Hwy. 14. From Stonehenge continue down the road about one mile to Maryhill Park.

Getting There: From Hood River, drive east on I-84 for 39.8 miles to Exit 104 and head across the bridge towards Yakima. Make a left at US-97 for 2.5 miles. Turn right on Hwy. 14 for 1.4 miles until Maryhill Loop Road. Turn left and drive to the parking lot and gate.

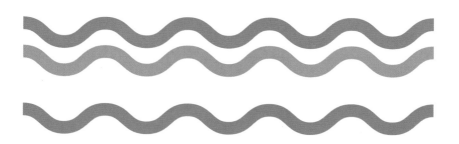

North Bonneville Trails

Bonneville, WA   **Easy**

12 miles of paved trails   **Year round**

North Bonneville hosts 12 miles of flat paved roads that are perfect for beginning bike riders. The bike path weaves around the community, like a suburban neighborhood. The roads are separate from cars and provide smooth flat rides for your little one. We like starting at the Bonneville Hot Spring Resort and Spa where you can have lunch or take in a swim (note: swimming is expensive and not always open to the public.) From the resort, pedal towards North Bonneville. The first half mile of the trail meanders around Kidney Lake before entering North Bonneville. Built in the late 1970s when the old town of Bonneville was demolished and became the Bonneville powerhouse, North Bonneville is quiet and centers around a golf course. Detour to play Frisbee golf, swing at the playground or munch on berries.

Getting There: Take I-84 west to Exit 44. Cross the Bridge of the Gods ($1 toll). Turn left on Hwy. 14, for 3 miles to Hot Springs Way. Turn right at the stop sign onto East Cascade Drive and follow for 1/2 mile to the Resort.

Photo by Ruth Berkowitz

Pedaling with Dad

The Dalles Riverfront

🅿️ **The Dalles, OR**   ① **Easy**

🏃 **8 miles of trail**

☀️ **Year round. Not protected from wind and sun.**

Ideal for young bikers, the Riverfront Trail is wide and flat and has interesting places to spot along the way. The trail will eventually span 10 miles from the Discovery Center to The Dalles Dam, but today, we have 8 miles to pedal. For the beginner, we suggest starting at what locals call "Pocket Park" formally known as Klindt Park. Head west past the Google Industrial Buildings. Along the way, look for the fishing platforms used for dip-netting salmon. Detour into Home at Last's Animal Shelter to play with their homeless dogs and cats. Stop at Chenowith Creek for fish-viewing and look for nibbled on wood, evidence of beavers. Look in the trees for nesting ospreys. By the time you reach the Discovery Center (which requires an uphill), you won't realize that you've logged 3.5 miles.

🧭 **Getting There:** Take I-84 east for 17 miles to Exit 82. Turn left on Chenowith Rd., and continue on River Rd. for 1.1. miles, then turn left on Klindt Dr. for .3 miles, to the parking lot. Public bathrooms. (541) 296-9533 • www.nwprd.org

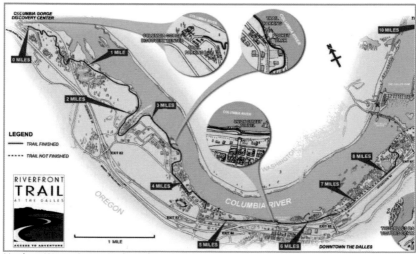

Northern Wasco County Parks and Recreation

Mountain Biking

Eight Mile Loop Trail

📍 **Area 44 Trails, Barlow Ranger District** ❷ **Moderate**
🚴 **6.2 mile loop** ◐ ☀ 🍁 **June-October**

Eight Mile Loop Trail is a fantastic single track for kids with a bit of stamina. Make sure to take the spur trail to Five Mile Butte Lookout where you can climb up the stairway of the lookout tower to get an eagle eye view of Mt. Hood and Mt. Adams. Zip downhill along the snaking single track back to the campground where you started. For little kids who are learning how to ride on dirt take the section that follows the creek as a shuttle. Kids and an adult can start at FR 4400-120 and gently descend to the Eight Mile Campground Day Use area where a car awaits.

🧭 **Getting There:** From Hood River, drive 26 miles south on Hwy. 35 until approximately .15 mile past milepost 71, and turn left on Dufur Mill Road (FR 44). Drive 10 miles and make a left on FR 4430. In .3 miles, you'll find Eight Mile Campground (FR 4430-150). Park at the trailhead in the day use area. The trail starts at the picnic area. NW Forest Pass required.

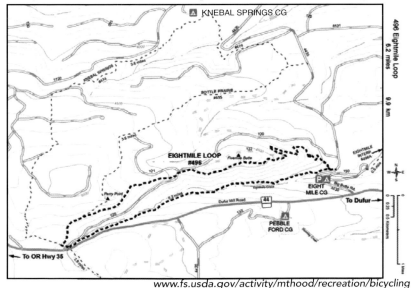

Knebal Springs Trail and Bottle Prairie

Area 44 Trails, Barlow Ranger District   **Moderate**
9 mile loop   **June-October**

This exhilarating loop ride is ideal for kids who are confident mountain bikers and ready to tackle a longer ride. Park at the Knebal Springs Campground and follow Knebal Springs up through an open forest for about 3.5 miles. Enjoy the fast, fun downhill to the trail junction with Bottle Prairie. Follow Bottle Prairie Trail up to Perry Point where you are rewarded with a long, swoopy single-track through the forest. Climb back up to the Campground to the car.

Getting There: From Hood River, drive 26 miles south on Hwy. 35 until approximately .15 mile past milepost 71, to Dufur Mill Road (FR 44). Turn left on FR 44 and travel 5.3 miles to FR 17 (signed for Knebal Springs Campground). Continue straight on FR 17 (FR 44 curves right). After 0.5 mile, take the right fork onto FS 1720, (signed for Knebal Springs) (FR 17 goes left). Stay on FR 1720 for 2.7 miles and turn right on FR 1720-150 and drive 0.2 mile to the entrance of Knebal Springs Campground. Bear left through the campground and park in the open grassy area on the left.
www.fs.usda.gov

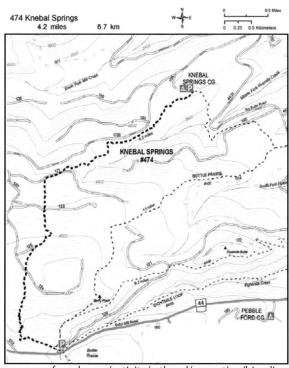

www.fs.usda.gov/activity/mthood/recreation/bicycling

Klickitat Rail Trail

Lyle, WA   **Moderate**

Varies; 31 miles from Lyle through Swale Canyon

Winter, spring and fall are best; Swale Canyon is closed in summer

Load your bikes and head to the Klickitat Rail Trail. A former railroad bed, the Klickitat Rail Trail follows the Klickitat River for 15 miles from Lyle to the town of Klickitat with another section of the trail beyond Klickitat that winds through Swale Canyon. For easiest access from the Gorge, we recommend parking at the area where Hwy 14 intersects with Hwy 142 just west of Lyle. At the parking area you'll find restrooms, a water fountain and an overlook of the Klickitat River. Follow the gravel trail up river through ponderosa pines, oak groves and, in the spring, wildflowers. The trail itself is an easy grade for beginners, but the gravel can be a bit loose for first timers without training wheels or balance bikes. In 1.6 miles up river, you'll find Fisher Hill Bridge which spans the river and allows you to pick up the trail on the west side of the river. Here the trail turns to single track, gets a bit more technical and continues all the way to the town of Klickitat. For younger riders or hikers, make your way .8 miles where a dirt road crosses the trail and heads down to the water. Follow this road downhill to access the river for rock throwing, wading and beach playing. Beware of poison oak along the banks and keep your eyes out for eagles and other wildlife.

If you make it all the way to the town of Klickitat, take a right on Main and 2nd St. until you reach the river. In the summer, locals challenge each other to jump off the cliff on the other side of the river. Cell phones might not work along the river so plan accordingly.

Getting There: Cross the Hood River Bridge into Washington and turn right on Hwy. 14. Drive 10.8 miles to Lyle. Before you come to town and after you cross the Klickitat, turn left on Hwy. 142. Take your first left into the parking lot.

Photo by Ruth Berkowitz

Crossing Fischer Bridge

51

😊 Post Canyon

🚲 *Hood River, OR*

②③ *Moderate to Extremely Difficult*

🏃 *Varies*

🌙☀️🍀 *Spring, summer, fall; can be too muddy in winter*

Known for its expert terrain and I-can't-believe-anyone-really-bikes-off-this-crazy-jump, Post Canyon has trails for all abilities, even beginners. For those who are just getting their wheels rolling, the area at the top of the hill called

Learning the skinnies

Photo by Peter Foley

Family Man has tamer teeter totters and skinnies. We like to start our adventure at Family Man which is accessible from Riordan Hill and play around on the stunts and pump tracks. We have a new Kleeway trail that is a good option for expert kids, especially those who bike up and down to Family Man from the Seven Streams Staging area. The trail is named in memory of Matt Klee, a local bike advocate and President of Hood River Area Trail Stewards. Matt tragically died biking at Whistler in 2014. Please give a special thanks to Matt as you watch your kids ride Lollipop Lane and learn to jump on the obstacles at Family Man. Matt advocated for these learn-to-ride features. Depending on ability, either ride down the Kleeway and get picked up from Seven Streams Staging Area or, from the Seven Streams Staging Area, ride up to Family Man on Seven Streams and back down the Kleeway. Another option is to start at Family Man and ride the more difficult Lower 8-Track. Our local bike shops have maps of the area and there's one posted at the entrance to Seven Streams. The trails are confusing and it's possible to get lost in the woods so pay attention.

Getting There: To Post Canyon, from Hood River drive south on Country Club Rd. for 1.6 miles, turn right on Post Canyon Rd. and follow the gravel road up to the Seven Streams Staging Area. To drive to Family Man, stay on Country Club and turn right on Riordan Hill Road. Follow Riordan 2.7 miles to the Family Man Staging Area.

Ski Bowl Ski Area
Government Camp, OR   Easy to Difficult
Varies   Summer

During the summer, Ski Bowl converts their ski resort into a premier mountain biking arena. You can bring your bike on a ski lift and then enjoy an exhilarating downhill ride. The terrain is full of single track and stunts. They offer guided rides, lessons, clinics and more. Leave your fear at home and bike with confidence. If you want to take a break from biking, head to their summer adventure park which has an alpine slide, rock walls, tree top action zone and much more.

Getting There: Take I-84 to Exit 64. Drive 38 miles on Hwy. 35 and continue on Hwy. 26 toward Portland. Ski Bowl is in Government Camp. (503) 272-3206 • www.skibowl.com/summer.

Syncline

Between Bingen and Lyle, WA   **Moderate to Difficult**
Varies   **Spring, Fall, Winter**

A geologic formation of basalt cliffs, the Syncline is one of the main places to mountain bike ride in the winter. The trails here reward riders with spectacular views, white oak savannahs, plenty of climbing and the infamous poison oak in the late spring and summer. The riding options are many, but for new pedallers, we advise starting them riding the old gravel road east from the parking area to the area where the dirt trail veers off to the left. Follow this trail up and get onto the jeep track and continue to climb up to the intersection with Little Maui. Turn east onto Little Maui and fly down the snaky single track through lush gullies and across trickling streams back to the bottom. There are technical areas on this trail that kids might need to dismount their bikes and walk. It's inspiring to watch one of the local experts ride the technical sections. There aren't really great maps of this area as much of the land is private property so pay attention and don't be afraid to stop another rider on the trail to ask directions. Yes, Dad, even men can ask directions!

Getting There: From Hood River, cross the bridge and head east on Hwy. 14 for 4.5 miles. Turn left onto Courtney Road and park in the new parking lot at the trailhead.

Photo by Peter Foley

Wyatt charging on Little Moab

Other Mt. Bike Trails

The Gorge has a number of expert trails for teens and adults. On the Oregon side, Whoopdee is one of our favorites. For a longer adventure, we like to ride Lewis River and The Plains of Abraham on Mt. St. Helens. Oh so many trails and so little time.

White Salmon Bike Park

White Salmon, WA ① ② ③ **Varies**

19 acres of trails and stunts ✳ **All seasons**

The White Salmon Bike Park is a prime example of a community pulling their resources together to turn an idea into reality. The community raised $20,000 in less than 30 days and began building a park on a wooded 19 acre piece of city land next to Jewett Creek which previously was a burn pile and unofficial dump. There are three different trails for young riders to link up and hone their skills. They can jump in the skills area and working on their balance skills on the skinnies. Trail map is located at the parking area on NE Tohomish next the the baseball fields.

Getting There: From Hood River, cross the bridge and turn right on Hwy. 14, then take the first right on Dock Grade Rd. At the top of the hill, turn left on Jewett. Turn right on NE Grandview Blvd., then left on NE O'Keefe Ave. Drive two blocks and turn right on NE Tohomish. Look for parking next to the ball fields or continue east on NE Tohomish to NE Park Avenue and turn left.

Balance Biking

Learning to ride a bike is a huge milestone. Gear and philosophy have changed in recent years with the introduction of balance bikes. Balance bikes are small, two-wheel bikes without training wheels or pedals. Toddlers use their legs to push along and eventually coast and balance with their feet perched on the

Photo by Nicole Faabourg

Josie nailing the skinny

bike frame. Balance bike proponents think that teaching kids to balance while coasting decreases the uneasy feelings that many kids have when their training wheels are removed. Amazingly, most kids who start with a balance bike skip training wheels completely. While many of the rides in the road and mountain bike section are good options for balance bikers, the following entries are ideal for balance bikers.

😊 Family Man

😊 Hood River   **❶ ❷ ❸ Varies**
🏃 Varies   **✳ All seasons**

Located on Hood River County Forestry lands, Family Man is a human built playground for bikers of all ages. Pump tracks, skinnies, teeter totters, dirt jumps you name it, Family Man has tons of stunts for experts and beginners. While your toddler may not be ready for the big jumps on Drop Out she will be delighted with Lolipop Lane or cruising around the big pump track with help or testing her balance walking on the skinnies or building forts in the woods. You get the picture. There's a lot to do here and pit toilets and a new parking area make it easy to post up for the afternoon while everyone in the family gets a ride in. In the summer, bring the family and hibachi on Wednesday nights for Families at Family Man. (See also Post Canyon above in Mountain Biking section.)

🧭 **Getting there:** From Hood River drive south on Country Club Rd. and turn right (west) on Riordan Hill Road. Follow Riordan 2.7 miles to the Family Man Staging Area.

Rolling the pumptrack

Photo by Paloma Ayala • www.fotoisphoto.com

Fort Cascades

😊 North Bonneville, WA   **❶ Easy**
🏃 1.5 miles   **✳ All seasons**

This 1.5 mile gravel trail is packed with history. Grab a map and follow the self guided tour along through the mossy boulders of this historic site. Once the

Area of a Native American village, the area was later populated by explorers, trappers, fishermen, settlers and railroad workers. Today, there isn't much left to see, but the numbered markers engaged one 5-year old enough to ride the whole trail looking for the interpretive signs. This trail is suitable for balance bikers or kids just learning to pedal on dirt.

Getting There: From Hood River drive west on I-84 to Cascade Locks. Cross the Bridge of The Gods ($1 toll), turn west on Hwy. 14 and drive just past the Bonneville Dam. On your left is the turn for Fort Cascades. Pit toilets and informational kiosk are at the trailhead.

Hood River Waterfront

Hood River   **Easy**

Varies   **All seasons**

Ellery cruising the waterfront

There are a variety of ways to ride the paved trail down on the waterfront but we recommend starting at the Hood River Inn and following the paved trail west between the hotel and the river. Little ones will marvel at riding under the Hood River Bridge. Follow the trail past the DMV and the marina where you can look at the boats then continue over the pedestrian bridge all the way to the Waterfront Park and The Hook. If you have a speedy rider, pay attention to the steep embankments next to the river. Combine this ride with a stop at the Hood River Historical Museum on the east side of the pedestrian bridge for a fun morning adventure.

Getting There: From Hood River drive east on I-84 to Exit 64 and head north towards the Hood River Bridge. Before the bridge, turn right on East Marina Way to the parking lot of the Hood River Inn. The trail starts behind the hotel.

Crossing the bridges

Indian Creek from Hood River High School

📍 **Hood River, OR**

② **Moderate**

🏃 **Varies**

☀ **All seasons**

This is a good introductory ride on dirt for young balance bikers or beginning pedalers. Start on the southwest corner of the track and head down the hill into the woods along Indian Creek. Turn right at the first Y and head towards the golf course. Help little ones navigate the few hills that exist but once settled in, they'll cruise along and find plenty of places to get off their bikes and explore, throw rocks and have a snack. Note that for safety reasons, you're not allowed to bike, hike or run on the golf course pathways.

🧭 **Getting There:** From Hood River turn south on 13th street and follow it 3 miles (13th turns into Tucker Rd.) turn right on Indian Creek Road at Windmaster Corner. The high school is on your left.

😀 Trillium Lake

📍 **Mt. Hood, OR**

① **Easy**

🏃 **2 miles on dirt**

☀ **Bike and hike spring/summer/fall; xc ski in the winter**

For a full, adventure packed day, head to the south side of Mt. Hood to Trillium Lake. The Day Use area hosts a stunning view of the mountain which on a clear day, reflects perfectly. You might recognize the scene since many expert photographers have captured Mt. Hood perfect reflection. Begin the flat, 2 mile dirt trail in either direction around the idyllic lake. The trail follows the banks of the lake, taking you over a variety of bridges through the wetlands and forest. Stick to the main path and you will return back to the Day Use

Riding with a view

Area and the parking lot. This area is a fun place to introduce riding on dirt for balance bikers and new riders. You might need to give your child a bit of extra help riding in a straight line over the bridges, but she will figure it out quickly. The more accomplished pedalers can stop and explore as they wait for their younger siblings or even plunge into the cold water.

Allocate plenty of time and pack snacks so you can stop along the way to look for salamanders, great blue herons and huckleberries in the fall. Looking for a multi sport day? Bring SUP's, fishing poles, inflatable boats, canoes, or anything else that doesn't have a motor. The lake is stocked regularly during the summer so fishing can be rewarding.

Getting There: From Hood River, head south on Hwy. 35 for 38 miles. Merge onto Hwy. 26 and look for the campground entrance on the left.

Other Options:

Other great options for balance biking include any of the skate parks during school hours when little kids have full access to the park. The paved portion of Catherine Creek and Balfour-Klickitat trail are also interesting options for young balance bikers with a lot of side exploring to do along the way.

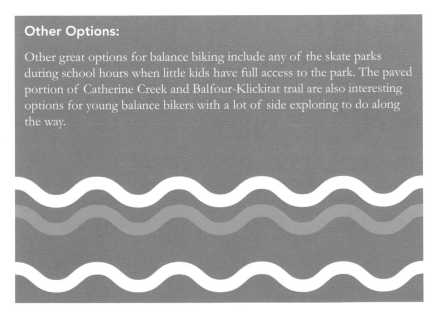

Learn to ride

Tips for teaching the Budding Biker:

• Temper your enthusiasm. Wait for your child to show an interest in riding. If you push her, she may get scared and refuse to ride.

• When selecting a bike resist the urge to buy a bike the child can grow into. Smaller is better because it helps children build confidence and skills. Also, look for the lightest bike you can find. Being able to pick the bike up—all by herself—is empowering.

• Make sure your child can put her feet down on the ground when sitting on her bike. This allows her to stay in control and be more independent.

• Reinforce safety by requiring helmets, teaching proper use of brakes and getting off the bike for curbs, busy roads and other obstacles.

• Start with pavement before dirt trails. Take the time to let your child get comfortable on pavement. Again, pushing children may scare them and create a barrier to enjoyment.

• Encourage your child to switch back and forth between a balance and pedal bike (with or without pedals). This will help her remember her confidence on the balance bike as she's learning to pedal the bigger bike. Fight the urge to stigmatize bikes as a "baby bike" and "big girl bike." Let your child pick her vehicle.

• Remember, riding is something fun for your child and has no room for parental ego. Children's interest vary. If you follow her lead and guide her gently, then you will create a rewarding, long-term family activity that everyone enjoys.

Try it again!

CHAPTER 4

Swimming Spots

FOR MERMAIDS AND MANATEES

Photo by Paloma Ayala • www.fotoisphoto.com

Looking to get your toes wet or get wet from head to toe, this section is for you. We have listed some prime places to cool off. You can plunge into a concrete swimming pool or adventure in the wild.

- Hood River Aquatic Center
- Kahneeta
- The Dalles Pool
- Water's Edge
- White Salmon Community Pool
- Hood River Marina

- Kingsley Reservoir
- Lost Lake
- Oneonta Gorge
- The Dalles Riverfront Park
- Tucker Bridge
- Wahtum Lake

Hood River Aquatic Center
Hood River, OR

This public swimming pool is one of Hood River's best assets. The center has three pools: a wading pool, a warm therapy pool, and a large lap pool. When the white tent covering the three pools opens up during the summer, you can swim with a view of Mt. Adams. Bigger kids can enjoy the rope swing, zipline and slide. The wading pool is ideal for the little ones be cause it's equipped with toys and is only 1½ feet deep. Best of all is the warm 90 plus degree therapy pool where kids can noodle around in the water for a long time without getting cold. The pool has kickboards, floaties, and more. You can buy swim goggles, swim diapers, but bring your own towels. They also offer swim lessons, kayak roll sessions and showers for grubby campers. Admission: 0-2 year olds, free; 3-17 and 60 years and up, $3.75; and 18-59 years olds, $4.75 for out of district visitors.

Getting There: From I-84 take Exit 62, drive east on Cascade Ave. and turn right on 13th St. until May St. Turn right and you will see the big white contraption. 1601 May St. (541) 386-1303 • www.hoodriverparksandrec.org

Photo by Hood River Aquatic Center

Kahneeta High Desert Resort
Warm Springs, OR

Eighty-five miles south of Hood River in the high desert, Kahneeta Resort is an ideal day-trip or an even better overnight. You can stay at the lodge, campground or in a TeePee. Owned by the Warm Springs Tribe, the resort has an outdoor double Olympic-size pool filled with natural hot springs mineral water. The pool is gently sloped, making it possible for young kids to stand up in the shallow area. The older kids will get their thrill on the 184-foot long water slide. For the adults, enjoy the hot tub, the deluxe European spa and perhaps even make a little money in the casino. Admission: $15.00 for 11 years and older; $10.00 for 4-10 year olds; and free for 4 and under.

Getting There: From Hood River, drive south on Hwy. 35 for 39 miles to Hwy. 26. Head east on Hwy 26 towards Bend/Madras and after 45 miles, turn left at Warm Springs Road. Follow signs for Kahneeta. Continue for 2.4 miles on Hwy. 8. 6823 Hwy. 8, Warm Springs
(800) 554-4786 • www.kahneeta.com

The Dalles Public Pool and Splash Park-Thompson Park
The Dalles, OR

Officially named The Northern Wasco County Aquatic Center, this 8 lane 50 meter pool opened in June 2015 and is an exciting addition to The Dalles. The pool attracts people from all sides of the Gorge. Kids can swim, swoosh down the 140 ft water slide and frolic on the 1800 sq ft splash pad. After swimming, check out the adjacent playground or hone your skills at the skatepark. So much to do – you could stay and play all day.

Getting There: Drive I-84 east of Hood River for 20 miles to Exit 83 and turn right. Turn left on W. 6th St. Turn left on Hostetler St. Turn right on W. 2nd St. 602 W. 2nd St., The Dalles
(541) 296-9533 • www.nwprd.org

Water's Edge at Lone Pine Village
The Dalles, OR

Though not a kid-centric place, Water's Edge Health and Wellness Center opens its saline lap and therapy pools to families on Saturdays from 1:00 to 4:00 pm. The new green-built club operated by Mid-Columbia Medical Center is an impressive facility with expansive windows overlooking the Columbia River, The Dalles Bridge and the Native American fishing platforms. Parents can take turns sweating in the sauna while the other adult supervises their young swimmers. Swim lessons are offered throughout the year. Another bonus is the Kids Club, which offers affordable childcare for members and non-members. Consider working out in their stellar fitness center prior to the public swim. After working up an appetite, stop at their on-site restaurant, The Bistro, and enjoy a healthy crepe, salad or panini. Fee: $5/adult and one child. $2.50/hour childcare.

Getting There: From Hood River drive east to Exit 87 and turn north at the off ramp. Turn left on Lone Pine Dr. Water's Edge is next to The Dalles Bridge. 551 Lone Pine Blvd., The Dalles (541)506-5779 • www.wellnessatwatersedge.com

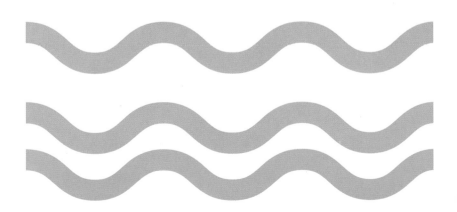

White Salmon Community Pool

In the heat of the summer, put on your swimsuit and hang out at this small community outdoor pool for splashy entertainment. Don't forget sunscreen and pool toys! Built in the 1930s, the pool helps you escape the hot sun and is ideal, especially if you want to swim outside or if you live in near by. Swim lessons offered. Check the website for days, times and costs.

Getting There: Cross the Hood River Bridge, turn left on Hwy. 14. Drive a fraction of a mile and turn right onto Dock Grade Rd. Turn left on Jewett Blvd. and right onto Main St. You'll find the pool right next to Whitson Elementary School. 160 NW Washington St.

(509) 493-1133 • www.ci.white-salmon.wa.us

White Salmon Pool 1948

Photo courtesy of City of White Salmon

Swimming Holes

In the summer, there's nothing more refreshing than plunging into one of our natural swimming holes. Here are some of our favorites.

Hood River Marina Park
🏊 *Hood River, OR*

This popular sandy beach on the Columbia River is a favorite place for kids to get their feet wet and it's a lso a way to avoid the hub-bub of the Event Site and the Spit. You can wade far from the shore in the shallow water, but please be aware of the current in the middle of the river. The grassy area has picnic shelters, BBQ pits, bathrooms and showers.

Photo by Brett VandenHeuvel

Getting There: From Hood River, take Exit 64 on I-84, head north to E. Port Marina Drive and turn left. Follow the road as it winds past the DMV and boat mooring to the parking area adjacent to the Columbia River. (541) 386-1645 • www.portofhoodriver.com

Kingsley Reservoir
🏊 *Hood River, OR*

Located nine miles from Hood River where the elevation is 3200 feet, this reservoir attracts swimmers, anglers, dirt bike and ATV enthusiasts and campers. You can wade easily since the shoreline is shallow and gradual, but watch out for barbed fish hooks. Many people fish from the dike just counter clockwise from the wooden pillars. Some like to do a mountain bike shuttle from here to Post Canyon. Beware, it can be windy and there's only one outhouse that needs to be upgraded.

Getting There: In Hood River, drive south on 13th St. which becomes Tucker Rd. Just past mile marker 4, turn right on Portland Dr. until Country Club Rd. Follow for about 9 miles until the reservoir. (541) 386-2616 • www.co.hood-river.or.us

67

Bryn Flying

Koberg Beach State Recreation Site

🅡 *Between Hood River and Mosier, OR*

From 1915 to about 1950, locals put on their dancing shoes and flocked to Koberg Beach. At that time, this was THE place to go. In its heyday, the dance hall had a live orchestra and the swimming facility well marked. All this disintegrated when the damming of the Columbia River altered the shoreline. The Hood River Historical Museum has photographs documenting the dancing days. Today the park remains a fun place to plunge into the river. Older kids especially like jumping from the cliff. Don't look Mom!

Getting There: From I-84, drive east to Exit 69 then double back west. Follow the signs for Koberg Beach near mile marker 66. Park and walk the trail on the west side of the big rock.

Swank swimsuits in 1935

😊 Lost Lake
📍 *Dee, OR*

This picturesque lake about 25 miles from Hood River is an all time favorite because it has so much to offer. You can swim in the freshwater lake, rent boats or SUPs and, our favorite, look for wiggling salamanders. Need some marshmallows for s'mores, head up to the General Store. Hike around the lake and you'll catch a memorable view of Mt. Hood. Some of the best swimming holes are located on the trail to the right of the store. As for the water, it's chilly and crystal clear. Remember to bring bug repellant. $6 entry fee.

🧭 **Getting There:** From Hood River, drive south on 13th St., which becomes Tucker Rd. Just past mile marker 5 make sure to stay right and follow the signs to Dee. Continue for another 14 curvy miles to Lost Lake. (541) 386-6366 • www.lostlakeresort.org

Photo by Ruth Burkowitz

Lake cruising

Oneonta Gorge

🐚 *Waterfall Alley, OR*

This crazy put-on-your-old-sneakers-and-get-wet adventure is ideal on a hot summer day. The less than one mile trail takes you inside the narrow gorge and to the bottom of a 100-foot waterfall. You begin by crossing a large pile of logs and hiking in water that can be two-to-four feet deep. Hand-holding and toddler-carrying involved. The hike is challenging, but possible with kids of all ages. Just don't tell Grandma!

Getting There: Drive I-84 to Ainsworth Park Exit 35. Continue west on the Old Hwy. 1.5 miles to the Horsetail Falls parking lot. (541) 386-2333 • www.fs.fed.us

Hang on!

Photo by Bethany Franger • www.blaineandbethany.com

The Dalles Riverfront Park

🐚 *The Dalles, OR*

When the temperatures rise over 100 degrees Fahrenheit, many folks congregate and swim at the Riverfront Park. The beach is sandy and the floating dock is a 100-yard swim from shore. There are lots of other diversions, including a playground and the Riverfront trail, a good place to bike. The Kayak Shack rents bikes, SUP's and kayaks.

Getting There: Take I-84 east to The Dalles to Exit 85. Turn left onto Brewery Overpass Road. Turn right on Riverfront Park Road. Park is ahead on your left.

Tucker Bridge/ Apple Valley
Hood River, OR

During the hot summer, head to Tucker Bridge for a refreshing dip in the cold river. You can access the river from the parking area across the street from Apple Valley Country Store. Be aware that the access trail is not suitable for very little kids and frail grandparents. The rope swing attached to the bridge attracts lots of locals on a hot summer day. The current can be strong, so beware, especially if you dare to swing into the frigid Hood River. It's a fun local spot which feels a bit like the shores in southern Georgia. People gather, drink ice tea and beer and plunge their bodies into the cold cold water. Good thing we don't have crocodiles.

Getting There: From Oak St., head south on 13th St., which becomes Tucker Rd. You'll see Apple Valley on the left and the unimproved parking pull out on the right.

Good summer fun

Photo by Robin Dickenson

Wahtum Lake

📍 Dee, OR

Looking for a less developed alternative to Lost Lake? Stop at Wahtum Lake. It's more challenging to access because of the 250 stair climb down to the lake but the "private" beaches along the lake edge make it worth it. Follow the Wahtum Express Trail 406J down to the lake's edge and wander as far as you like, literally, since this is the Pacific Crest Trail. If you venture here in late August or early September, you'll find thimbleberries and huckleberries and not as many mosquitoes as other times of the year. We saw tons of crawdads on the north end of the lake next to area where the logs pile up. For the fisher-people in your family, the lake is stocked with trout. If you are really keen, hike the .7 miles to the summit of Chinidere Mountain, arguably one of the best views of the Mark O. Hatfield Wilderness Area. You can also hike 13 miles down to Eagle Creek. Some backcountry campsites exist around the lake and there are a few drive up sites at the trailhead that include a pit toilet, fire rings and picnic tables. Be aware the elevation is 3732 feet, so it can be chilly at night, even in the summer. Parking fee is $5/day or display your Northwest Forest Pass. The wilderness regulations are strict here so be aware of what's allowed and what's not. Mainly, no more than 12 heartbeats per group so pick another spot if you have a large group.

Getting There: From Hood River drive south on Tucker Road to the Dee Hwy. In Dee, turn right and cross the river. Follow the signs to Lost Lake, but turn right after 4.9 miles. Continue on the narrow forest road for 4.3 miles. At FR 1310, drive 6 miles to the trailhead. Park and walk down the stairs to the lake. Day use fee $5.00, camping $10.00.

For other places to get wet, consider Doug's Beach, Horsethief Lake, Toll Bridge Park and Tucker Park.

Tips for Swimming

Buddy Up: Always good to have your child pick a buddy to swim with so they can keep an eye on each other.

Beware of Current: The current can be strong in the Columbia and in other local rivers, especially in the middle of the river. Try not to swim against the current's pull, instead swim perpendicular to it.

Life Jacket Law: Children 12 and under must legally wear a life jacket when on a boat that is moving, including a raft or SUP.

Learn CPR and Rescue Techniques: Hopefully you won't have to use it, but it's always helpful to have these skills. Contact Hood River Community Education for classes.

Swim Lessons:
Hood River Aquatic Center, Hood River Sports Club, White Salmon Pool, The Dalles Fitness and Court Club, Northern Wasco County Aquatic Center.

ZEBRAS, ALPACAS & STURGEON...

Oh My!

Want a bite?

Oodles of critters live freely in the Gorge. There are also many farms where children can pet and feed these creatures. As you kid around, you will spy alpacas, eagles, sturgeons and maybe even a zebra. Below are some of the places where we love to find animals.

- Alpacas
- Bonneville Fish Hatchery
- County Fairs
- Eagles at the Klickitat
- Exotic Birds
- Salmon Swimming
- Schreiner Farms

Alpacas
📍 Hood River, OR

Cousins of the llama, alpacas first came to the United States in 1984 from South America. Today, it's illegal to import alpacas, and as a result, breeding alpacas has become a lucrative business. Cascade Alpaca Farm has photogenic alpacas which you can feed. Listen to the babies hum to their mothers and each other. Each baby has a unique hum. Alpacas have a gentle personality, as soft as their fur. In their yarn store, you can see a real spinning wheel and learn how to spin the soft wool into yarn. There are two different types of alpacas: the Huacaya with fluffy and crimpy fleece and the rarer Suri with silky pencil looking locks. The Enchanted Alpaca store in downtown Hood River sells alpaca products, including teddy bears and exquisite coats for mom—don't you think everyday should be Mother's Day?

Getting There: Drive south on Hwy. 35 for 8.5 miles until Central Vale Road. Turn right and continue to Sylvester Dr. Make your way up the hill to Cascade Alpacas Farm. 4207 Sylvester Dr., Hood River (541) 354-3542 • www.foothillsyarn.com

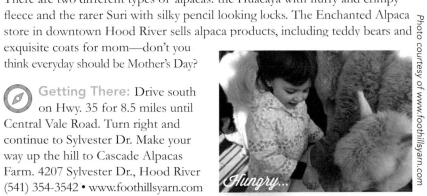

Hungry...

Photo courtesy of www.foothillsyarn.com

Bonneville Fish Hatchery and Dam Fun
Waterfall Alley and N. Bonneville

You can look a massive sturgeon in the eye at the largest fish hatchery in Oregon. The oldest and largest living creatures in the Columbia River, sturgeon came into this world before the dinosaurs. Make sure to find 70-plus year-old Herman, the famous ten foot long fish, weighing more than 450 pounds. Fortunately, he wasn't stolen in 2007, when someone (probably a number of people) managed to sneak into the Hatchery and take six sturgeon in the middle of the night. The case was never solved. You can also feed the trout and salmon. During spawning season, you can watch the biologists harvest the eggs and sperm from the fish, but this might be disturbing for young children. We love to watch the shimmering salmon jump out of the water and catapult themselves over the 5-foot wall. It's also worth your while to explore the Bradford Island Visitor Center and view salmon swimming up the ladders and learn about hydropower. For even more fish and dam fun, you can drive across the Bridge of the Gods to the Washington Shore Visitor Complex and see the inner workings of the dam. In the early fall, look for the boisterous sea lions feasting on salmon. It's fun to watch them catch salmon, but many folks find them to be trouble and have tried a number of ways (even shooting them!) to stop the sea lions from eating the salmon.

Getting there: Take I-84 to Exit 40 (approximately 4 miles west of Cascade Locks, OR) For the fish hatchery, bear left at the flagpole intersection and follow the road around to the large parking lot on the left. For the Bradford Island Visitor Center, bear right at the flagpole intersection and follow the signs for approximately one mile along park roads.

Bradford Island Visitor Center operated by US Corp of Army Engineers • (541) 374-8820
www.nwp.usace.army.mil

Bonneville Fish Hatchery, operated by OR Department of Fish and Wildlife • (541) 374-8393
www.dfw.state.or.us

Humongous Ancient Herman

Photo by Blaine Franger www.blaineandbethany.com

County Fairs

🧭 *Hood River, OR and Stevenson, WA*

Thanks to the 4H kids, the County Fairs are the ultimate animal adventure. You'll see horses, pigs, alpacas, chickens, bulls, guinea pigs, sheep, rabbits, geese, mice, turkey and more. The young competitors tend to their animals and are usually happy to let you play with them. Many families camp out at the fair all weekend. Don't miss the 4-H competitions. You will be surprised how tame the chickens and goats can be. Go early in the day to hang with the animals. Then return in the afternoon for an amusement ride, a performance and yummy fair food, like the super sweet elephant ears. The Hood River County Fair occurs in late July every summer.

Getting There: Drive south on Hwy. 35 for 4.8 miles, turn right on Dethman Ridge Rd, then right on WyEast Rd. until you reach the fairgrounds. 3020 Wy'East Rd., Hood River
(541) 354-2865 • www.hoodriverfair.org

The Skamania County Fair and Timber Carnival is held at the Stevenson Fairgrounds in mid-August. This fair is the only fair in the state of Washington and Oregon that does not charge admission to enter. For a nominal fee, you can enter the timber contest and test your skills at axe throwing and log rolling.

Getting There: From Hood River, drive east on I-84 to Cascade Locks, Exit 44, cross the Bridge of the Gorge and turn right on Hwy. 14.
710 Rock Creek Dr., Stevenson
www.skamaniacounty.org

Duck, duck, goose...

Eagles at the Klickitat
🦅 Lyle, WA

Photo by Jurgen Hess

About 165 bald eagles spend the winter in the Gorge and the number has been increasing over the years. Eagles were almost extinct in the 1970s because of the widespread use of the poisonous DDT pesticide. Since that's been prohibited, eagles are making a comeback.

Many of these magnificent birds migrate from the north and west and congregate around the lower Klickitat Canyon where they feast on the salmon swimming upriver to spawn and die. Bring your binoculars, patience and eagle eyes. From the parking area, follow the .7 mile stroller friendly paved trail. Look for the birds perched in the trees or soaring in the sky. Wonder why they are called bald eagles but aren't really bald? In old English, "bald" means white. Even more confusing, young eagles have dark brown heads, but after four or five years, their feathers change and become bright white.

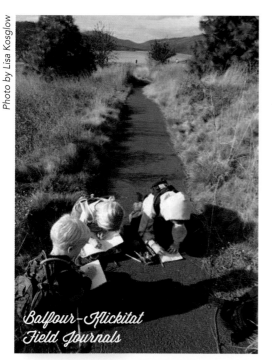

Photo by Lisa Kosglow

Balfour–Klickitat Field Journals

Getting There: To the Balfour Trailhead, cross the Hood River Bridge and turn right/east on Hwy. 14. Drive 10 miles and turn left at the sign for Appleton, milepost 75.9. The trailhead is .2 miles up the road. You can also spot eagles on the eastside of the Klickitat on the Rail Trail.

Exotic Birds

🐦 *Hood River, OR*

At James' Organic Blueberry Farm, you not only have the benefit of picking blueberries, but can also come face-to-face with a Ugandan Crane. Marvel at her golden mohawk and bright colorful head. Nature has an amazing palette of colors! The chickens have fanciful roosting homes, like a pink church and an old fashioned country store. Artist and owner Ted James loves birds, and is thrilled to share his passion and knowledge! You can stop by most of the summer to see the birds and blueberries ripen in July. Call for hours.

🧭 **Getting There:** From the middle of Hood River, drive up 13th St. to Belmont St. Make a right for almost 3 miles, then a right on Methodist Road. 1190 Methodist Road, Hood River • (541) 386-5806

Have you seen Big Foot?

Did you know that Skamania County has the highest documented sightings of Big Foot? This large, hairy hominoid might be surviving somewhere in the Gorge. There's a law in the county that prohibits shooting Big Foot, also known as "Sasquatch" or "wild man." To learn more, see www.bfro.net and if you see him, please take a picture for our next book … let us know if he speaks English.

Salmon Swimming and Spawning

Various Places in the Gorge

We have a number of fish hatcheries scattered throughout the Gorge, and they're especially interesting to visit when the salmon spawn in the fall. Magically, salmon know where home is after they've been out in the ocean for a few years. The largest of the Pacific Salmon, the Chinook can weigh up to 40 pounds—that's more than a young child. We like to visit the Spring Creek Hatchery in White Salmon, and watch the salmon jump high into the air as they catapult themselves up the fish ladders.

Another place to watch the salmon in the wild is near the Fisher Hill Bridge on the Klickitat River. You can walk to the edge of the canyon and see the salmon leaping up the river to spawn. You might also see some of the Native American fishermen using their long dip nets to scoop the salmon. Please respect their ancient fishing rights and avoid climbing on their platforms.

A walk up Eagle Creek in Waterfall Alley is another interesting place to watch the salmon spawn. Here, the salmon swim in the shallow water and you can practically touch them. It's a little sad, almost like a fish graveyard but it's part of the circle of life and will probably generate some interesting questions from your little ones.

Getting There: Spring Creek Fish Hatchery: 61552 State Road 14 Underwood, WA 98651; 509-493-1730. Fisher Hill Bridge: (see Klickitat Rail Trail.) Eagle Creek: Take I-84 west to Exit 41. Turn left and head to the parking area and trailhead.

Photo by Stephen Datnoff • www.datnoff.com

Spawning Salmon

Schreiner Farms

📷 *Dallesport, WA*

Not too many people know about this private farm, and we recommend it if you find yourself on the Washington side of the Gorge and need a little excursion. It feels like you're on an African Safari. The road is less than one mile and visitors are asked to stay in their vehicles. From your car, you can see elk, camels, giraffes, yaks, wallaroos and zebras. Yes, that's right -- zebras in the Gorge! If you are lucky, some of the animals may be grazing near the fence. You might want to double this outing with a hike at Horsethief Lake State Park or an adventure to Maryhill's Stonehenge, a full size replica of the real Stonehenge.

🧭 **Getting There:** Cross the Hood River Bridge, turn right on Hwy. 14 for 18.7 miles and turn right on Schreiner Farms Rd. www.schreinerfarms.com

Chomp, chomp, chomp...

Photos by Jurgen Hess

CHAPTER 6

Hanging out

IN THE ORCHARD

Photo by Margot Angstrom

Bears love plums

Grab your bucket and start picking. Summer and Fall in the Gorge means fresh fruits and vegetables. There's nothing tastier than picking and eating food straight from the source. Here in the Gorge, our farms grow some of the best tasting fruit in the world. Our mouths are watering just thinking about it!

- Apples
- Blackberries
- Blueberries
- Cherries
- Huckleberries
- Lavender
- Pears
- Pumpkins
- Strawberries and Raspberries

 # Apples

☀ ❀ Harvest Season: August-November

Apples have been growing in the Hood River Valley since the 1850s when Nathaniel and Mary Coe planted the first trees. Since then, they have become one of the most popular fruit farmed in the Gorge. Some orchards, like Kiyokawa Family Orchards, grow their apples on low trees that look like bushes making it easy for kids to pick their own apples. When you pick, hold onto the apple and twist gently. If ripe, the apple falls off easily. Many of the orchards, like Draper's Farm, have a cold storage facility, allowing you to buy from them all year long.

Can I have a bite?

Photo courtesy of Kiyokawa Orchard

Draper's Farm: Grow a variety of apples plus sell delicious non-pasteurized apple cider. Kids can also play with their farm animals. Always open!
6200 Hwy. 35, Mt. Hood • (541) 352-6625 • www.drapergirlscountryfarm.com

Kiyokawa Family Orchards: A favorite because they grow 97 different types of apples and have the largest u-pick area in the Gorge. Make sure to chomp into the Mt. Rose apple - it's green on the outside bright pink inside! They also host a number of special kid centered events with tractor rides, pinatas and music. Dogs are allowed, but must be on leash.
8129 Clear Creek Rd., Parkdale • (541) 352-7115 • www.mthoodfruit.com

Mt. Hood Organic Farm: The first organic farm in the valley kindly donates part of their crop to School Aid, a program in partnership with local markets, schools and the Oregon Food Bank. You can come buy apples from their farm early October until early February. We like lounging in the grass, crunching an apple and admiring one of the most stunning views of Mt Hood in the area. Guests from out of town? Steer them towards the cozy cabins for rent adjacent to the orchard. 7130 Smullin Dr, Mt Hood, OR 97041
(541) 352-7123 • www.mthoodorganicfarms.com

Mt. View Orchards: Hosts special events on the weekends with hay rides and apple cider. They have several play areas for kids and unlike many of the other orchards, they welcome leashed dogs.
6670 Trout Creek Ridge Rd., Parkdale
(800) 529-6554 • www.mtvieworchards.com

Gorging on berries

Blackberries

☀ ❄ *Harvest Season: July-September*

Many call Blackberries nasty weeds and you might laugh that they're even listed in our book. It's true—blackberries are prolific and can take over your yard. Moreover, picking blackberries can be painful because of their prickly thorns. Nevertheless, we still love eating them, especially with ice cream or in homemade pie. If they don't grow in your yard or your neighbor's yard, then wander into the wild. The tastiest berries grow near a water source, but away from busy roads where exhaust fumes or herbicides can contaminate the fruit. Here is one place we like to harvest.

Beacon Rock State Park-Doetsch Day Use Area: This one mile flat paved trail loops along the Columbia and the old Doetsch Ranch site and has fantastic berry picking opportunities, especially on the west side. We like to take bikes and grandparents so kids can bike as adults pick berries. Cross Hood River Bridge, turn left on Hwy. 14 and continue to Beacon Rock. About one mile past the Beacon Rock parking lot, turn left on Doetsch Ranch Road and then right into large parking area and trailhead. Bathrooms and water at parking area.

 Blueberries

🌑 ☀ ❄ *Harvest Season: June to September*

Blueberries might be the best fruit to pick with young children because they don't have seeds, and most of the bushes are low enough for kids to fill their own bucket. High in antioxidants, blueberries are one of the most nutritious fruits and also help ward off cancer, aging and heart disease. Blueberries grow in clusters and do not ripen at the same time. The best time to pick is early in the morning or the evening when it's cooler and the berries are more flavorful at this time. Pick the blue ones and leave the red and green ones for your next visit. We like picking on Methodist St. at both of the blueberry farms: Juicy Blue and James' Organic Blueberries. The later has pheasants, cranes and chickens. While picking, let your imagination roam, just like the James' chickens.

Photo by Nicole Faabourg

Blueberry eyes

Browning Blueberries: 5164 Imai Rd., Hood River • (541) 354-3760

James' Organic Blueberries: A favorite place to come, pick organic berries and look at Ted's amazing exotic birds. • 1190 Methodist Road, Hood River • (541) 386-5806

Juicy Blue U-Pick Berry Farm: The owners of this non-certified organic farm encourage families to come with a picnic and the farm also grows other berries, including Haskap berries from Japan, that are longer in size, more tart in taste, and contain three times the amount of antioxidants. You can also pick their currants which grow in abundance. Late summer hours, usually 9 to 9, but call to check. •1206 Methodist Road, Hood River • (541) 340-9607

Two Peaks Blue: (certified organic)
5000 O'Leary Rd., Odell • (541) 354-1706

Wilinda's Blueberry Patch: With 12 different
varieties of blueberries, the season starts early and
ends late. The farm also sells woven baskets to fund
special surgeries in Uganda.
730 Frankton, Hood River • (801) 556-7964

Cherries

☀ **Harvest Season: June to July**

We have incredible tasting cherries in the Gorge. However, picking cherries with little kids can be more challenging than some of the other fruits around, especially if your kids don't know how to spit out the cherry pits. Some orchards forbid children from climbing the ladders that make it easier to reach the cherries. When you pick, look for cherries that are plump and ripe and if you keep the stem on the fruit, they keep longer. Cherries don't ripen off the tree. There are many varieties—from Bings to Vans to the delicious Queen Anne cherries. If you become a cherry enthusiast, it may be prudent to buy a cherry pitter. Try freezing your cherries, pit and all. We also love drying cherries and then dipping them in chocolate—yum! The Hood River Valley hosts a cherry festival during peak season where you'll find more cherry ideas, including lots of jams.

Filling the bucket

Photo by Kaori Stewart

Evans Brothers Cherry Farm: A favorite place to pick cherries with acres to choose from and a stellar view.
701 State St., Mosier
(541) 478-3550
www.evansfruit.com

Hood River U-Pick Cherries: Has a fun picnic place where you can pick cherries and picnic with double mountain view. The farm also grow other fruits and vegetables, including apples, raspberries, blueberries, garlic, kale, tomatoes, and flowers.
4320 Royal Anne Dr., Hood River
(541) 359-4481
www.hoodriverupick.com

Idiot's Grace Organic Cherries: We filled our freezer last year with the delicious organic cherries from this farm, so plump and tasty, refreshing in a winter smoothie and fabulous right off the tree.
8450 Hwy. 30, Mosier • (541) 490-5249

Huckleberries

Photo by Lisa Kosglow

☀ ❄ *Harvest Season:*
August - September

Grizzly bears love them; Huck Finn may have been named after them; and farmers have been unable to grow them. When you search for and find these plump huckleberries, you can imagine the Native Americans doing the same. Similar to blueberries, huckleberries are a deep purple color and a little smaller in size. Most wild huckleberry fields grow in higher elevations. Before you search, you might want to sample a huckleberry shake at the Apple Valley Country Store on Tucker Rd., Mikes' Ice Cream in Hood River, or at the city of Bingen's annual huckleberry festival in September.

Can't get enough

Elk Cove at Cloud Cap: This kid-friendly 3.8 mile trail off of Cloud Cap has fields of huckleberries and wildflowers, not to mention a fabulous view of Mount Hood.

Gifford Pinchot National Forest Huckleberry Fields (or Sawtooth Berry Fields): It is worth the bumps over the washboard dirt roads to get to this area. You are allowed to pick on one side of the road as the other side is exclusively for Native Americans. Check with the Ranger Station for status of berry ripeness and rules. www.fs.fed.us/gpnf

Tea Cup Lake: This popular cross country area has wild huckleberries growing along the trail.

Wahtum Lake: Not only a fun place to hike and swim, but home to buckets of huckleberries.

Lavender

◐ ◈ ✿ *Harvest Season: June to September*

Head to the lavender fields for some sweet smelling flowers or lavender lotion. Not only aromatic and therapeutic (it relieves burns, bites, headaches, sore muscles and has other healing powers), lavender can also flavor your food, either sweet on ice cream, or savory on lamb. Here in the Gorge, we have a number of lavender farms growing gorgeous flowers, but also producing their own lavender products. Beware of bees buzzing around the fields—usually they're so full of nectar that they won't sting you.

Photo by Melanie McCloskey

Flowers make kids smile

Hood River Lavender: Located on a steep hill overlooking both Mt. Hood and Mt. Adams, this farm grows more than 60 varieties of organic lavender. They host a yearly festival where you can make lavender wands—a perfect present for Grandma.
3801 Straight Hill Rd.,
Hood River
(888) Lav-Farm
www.hoodriverlavender.com

Hoffman Hills Lavender: (closed Sundays) Come visit the lavender farm and pick your own varieties. The farm also hosts weddings and other events.
6140 Mill Creek Rd.,
The Dalles
(541) 288-6060
www.hoffmanhillslavender.com

Riversong Sanctuary: This farm has a wonderful history and used to be an idyllic school for young 5 to 8 year olds. Today, the 91-acre farm grows lavender, vegetables and medicinal herbs. They encourage visitors to pick lavender and picnic in their newly built stone grotto area. Open Wednesday to Sunday from 11 to 5, there's a Farm Stand selling fresh food.
3226 Dee Highway, Odell • (541) 354-9909 • www.riversongsanctuary.com

Pears

☀ ❀ *Harvest Season: August to October*

There's nothing tastier than a perfectly ripened Comice pear (except maybe ice cream or chocolate). Indeed, pears are flavorful, not to mention healthy. Our area grows more than half of the country's winter pears (Anjou, Bosc and Comice), and we produce 11 percent of all the United States' Bartlett pears. Some pears like Starkrimson do not ripen well on the tree and need to be picked ahead of time. However, the Anjou or Bartlett's can be plucked and eaten right from the tree. To properly pick a pear (can you say that fast?), hold the pear and twist so that the stem separates easily from the branch. If you want your pear to ripen quickly, place it in a brown paper bag with a banana. The banana releases ethylene gas that makes a pear ripen. Besides eating them fresh or in pies, try dipping pears in chocolate or thinly slicing them for salads. Just pearfect!

Draper Girls Country Farm: This farm is busy with a variety of u-pick fruit, including pears.
6200 Hwy. 35, Mt. Hood • (541) 352-6625 • www.drapergirlscountryfarm.com

Kiyokawa Family Orchards: One of the oldest farms in the area and our favorite places to pick fruit with an idyllic setting and a very organized u-pick process. 8129 Clear Creek Rd., Parkdale • (541) 352-7115 • www.mthoodfruit.com

Mt. Hood Organic Farms & Garden Cottages: You can't pick the pears here, but you can buy fruit from the farm or even stay in their cozy cottages. It's also fun to walk around the orchards and explore.
7130 Smullen Rd., Mt. Hood • www.mthoodorganicfarms.com

Pumpkins

❀ *Harvest Season: October*

Halloween hails as one of our favorite kid holidays and that means the annual pilgrimage to the Pumpkin Farm. Our rule is that the kids have to be able to carry the pumpkin they choose. Many of the pumpkin patches host oodles of Halloween activities and people in the Gorge love to celebrate Halloween. Downtown Hood River goes all out with businesses staging haunted houses and trick or treating. Kids used to pick pumpkins at Rasmussen's Farm, but that recently closed and might have new owners in the near future. In the meantime, you may have to head to The Dalles for pumpkin fun.

Renken Farms: Don't let the crowd scare you away when you pull into the parking area during the farm's Halloween festivities. These homesteaders from the 1800's keep folks entertained with a wide range of activities from face painting to tractor rides to, my personal favorite, pumpkin launching with an enormous slingshot. Sip fresh pressed cider or munch on sweet elephant ears. Prices are reasonable with most activities in the $1 to $2 range, and the long lines move quickly. Please check their website for special events like Belly Dancing, choir music and high school Jazz concerts.
3050 Three Mile Rd., The Dalles
(541)-296-3024
www.renkenfarms.com

Photo by Brett VandenHeuvel

Riley in the drivers seat

Strawberries and Raspberries

⊙ ☀ ❀ Harvest Seasons: June to September

In the 1890s, strawberries grew prolifically throughout the Hood River Valley and many won impressive awards. Today, there are less strawberries and more apples and pears. The farm grown strawberries have much more flavor than the commercially grown ones. Sample some yourselves!

The Gorge White House: This elegant orchard has u-pick raspberries, and strawberries as well as dahlias to cut and bring home to Mom. The setting, with the double mountain view, beckons artists to come paint the scene. Enjoy a glass of wine or house made hard cider while your kids munch on berries. For substantial food options grab something from the food cart on the patio. Although owned by the other Kennedy Family, we're sure Jackie O would have loved this farm.
2265 Hwy. 35, Hood River • (541)-386-2828 • www.thegorgewhitehouse.com

Hood River U-Pick: Golden and red raspberries for picking.
4320 Royal Anne Dr., Hood River • (541) 359-4481 • www.hoodriverupick.com

The motherload

Photo by Paloma Ayala • www.fotoisphoto.com

Market is open!

Gorge Grown, our local foodshed advocacy group, promotes food issues and connects farmers, consumers, chefs, educators and local food enthusiasts. In addition to hosting farmers markets around the Gorge, they also publish a yearly publication called, "Who's Your Farmer." Well used and dog eared at our home, this comprehensive guide along with the Gorge Grown website, help you find local, farm fresh produce, like fresh cheese, eggs, chickens and produce. Pick up a hard copy at any of the visitor centers or farmers markets or check out the digital version on the www.gorgegrown.com website.

Other U-pick Opportunities

Annie's Apricots: Tasty apricots color the trees of this small farm located two miles east of Mosier on Hwy. 30. Look for the sign on the right. Harvest of these "orbs of sunshine" is mid-July and only lasts for a few weeks. Make sure to call ahead. 8264 Hwy. 30, Mosier (541) 348-3502

Draper Girls Country Farm: In addition to apples and pears, the farm grows peaches, plums, and nectarines. They often have sheep and other animals hanging around the farm.
6200 Hwy. 35, Mt. Hood • (541) 352-6625 • www.drapergirlscountryfarm.com

Photo by Blaine Franger • www.blaineandbethany.com

Tips for Picking

• Pack hats and sunscreen

• Call the farm to find out if the fruit is ripe and ready to pick.

• Avoid washing picked fruit until you are ready to eat it. Washing fruit prematurely makes it apt to spoil quicker.

Photo by Robin Dickenson

• Some fruit, like cherries and blueberries, are best picked in the morning.

• Leave your pets at home.

• After harvesting, keep your fruit in a cool place. Consider bringing a cooler.

• For the keen fruit lover, buy a vacuum sealer and dehydrator to preserve the bounty for the winter.

Full buckets

Fun Food Activities

Our fertile soil combined with hard working, innovative farmers equates to some of the best fruit and vegetables in the world. Eating local especially in the summer and fall is easily possible. Here are some ways to know your farmer.

Fruit Festivals: The Hood River Valley hosts several fruit festivals, including Blossom Festival (April), Cherry Days (July), Apple Days (August), Pear Celebration (September), Heirloom Apple Days (October) and Harvest Festival (October). www.hoodriver.org

Farmers' Markets: We have a number of farmers' markets around the Gorge. Hood River (Thursday 4-7), Mosier (Sunday 4-7), Odell (Saturday 10-2), Stevenson (Saturday 10-1), The Dalles (Tuesday 11-2), Trout Lake (Saturday 9-3), White Salmon (Tuesday 4-7). Please check gorgegrown.com, to confirm time and place. Note that when you shop at a grocery store, 18% of your purchase money goes to the farmer, but when you buy at the farmers' market, 90% goes to the farmer.

Community Supported Agriculture (CSA's): Some farms offer memberships in exchange for regular deliveries of their produce. With a CSA you invest in the farm and reap the benefits of the harvest. Take a look at Gorge-Grown.com for a list of CSAs.

Hood River Fruit Loop: For information about local farms, pick up a Hood River Fruit Loop Map or find one at www.hoodriverfruitloop.com.

Gorge Grown: The website, www.Gorgegrown.com, has tons of information on eating local and getting to know your farmer and your food.

Fruit Heritage Museum: Located in The Fruit Company's packing house, the Fruit Museum details the history of the fruit industry. You can see a 1930s pickers cabin and learn about the struggles and rewards of farming. The Fruit Company opens its doors to locals on Friday when they sell reduced cost fruit and other gourmet goodies that did not make it into their delicious gift baskets. 2900 Van Horn Dr., Hood River • www.thefruitcompany.com

CHAPTER 7

PROMISING
Picnic Places

Photo by Paloma Ayala • www.fotoisphoto.com

So hungry...

Fresh air, a scenic quiet place to run around and tasty food lead to a successful outing. You can picnic almost anywhere, especially in most of the areas described in our book. This chapter lists some of our favorite picnic spots, ones that are easily accessible. Bring a ball, some bubbles, and maybe a few other toys. If you don't want to chomp on sand, remember to pack the peanut butter & jelly sandwiches and other gourmet items!

- Dog Creek Waterfall
- Doug's Beach State Park
- Maryhill Winery
- Rooster Rock State Park
- Starvation Creek
- Stratton Gardens
- Tucker Park

Dog Creek Waterfall

㉑ Skamania, WA

Exploring Dog Creek

We love picnicking here on a hot day in front of the 30-foot cascading waterfall. The gushing water is only 100 feet from the gravel parking area, so it's quickly satisfying for the little ones who don't want to hike and are eager to get wet before or after lunch. The stream provides lots of diversions. Look for the tiny fish swimming around. But beware of the overly adventurous ones like local author Scott Cook who scrambles up the rocks to even more waterfalls or maybe some pokin' around—so stay away from that area.

Getting There: Cross the Hood River Bridge, turn left on Hwy. 14 and continue for 9.2 miles. You'll see the sign for Dog Creek, just past milepost 56.

Cooling down at Dougs

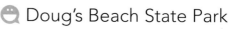 Doug's Beach State Park
Dallesport, WA

Known primarily as a windsurfing spot, and we advise steering clear when the winds blow, but on calm days this beach situated under the basalt cliffs makes you feel like you're on the Big Island in Hawaii. The rocks are sprinkled with mulberry shade trees, plums and blackberries making this a late summer bonanza of free fruit picking. Play on the beach under the trees or follow the trail on the east side over a rocky hill to a smaller "private" sandy beach with a picnic table. In the summer, look for the nesting osprey family. The park has some picnic tables and a pit toilet. If you venture off the riverbank keep an eye out for poison oak.

Getting There: From Hood River, cross the bridge and turn right on Hwy. 14. Drive 15 miles until milepost 79. You'll see the long parking area on the south side of the highway. Park here and hold hands as you help kids cross the tracks at the railroad crossing area to the park. Discover Pass required. (509) 773-3141 • www.parks.wa.gov

Maryhill Winery
Goldendale, WA

Located 40 miles from Hood River, the Maryhill winery has award winning wines, and panoramic views. The winery doesn't serve lunch, but they encourage guests to enjoy the view and picnic at their tables. Bring your own picnic or purchase food at their well stocked deli. They have a huge outdoor amphitheater for live concerts, which is also ideal for running around and creating your own spontaneous performance.

Getting There: Take I-84 east to Exit 104, Yakima/Bend. Turn right on US-97N, then left on Hwy. 14. The winery is on the river side. 9774 Hwy. 14, Goldendale • (877) 627-9445 • www.maryhillwinery.com

Rooster Rock State Park

🅐 Corbett, OR

Located at the so called "Gateway into the Gorge," Rooster Rock State Park has dozens of picnic tables beckoning families to gather for a picnic and perhaps even a plunge in the River. You'll find covered shelters, BBQ grills, and a number of stairways down to the water, including a boat ramp. Be warned the park hosts two clothing optional beaches on the farthest east side. Toss a frisbee at one of their two disc golf courses.

Getting There: From I-84 take Exit 25/Rooster Rock. The off-ramp leads straight to the park's tollbooth ($5 day use fee). (800) 559-6949 • www.oregonstateparks.org

Starvation Creek

🅐 Hood River, OR

This rest area offers a shady picnic by a waterfall that's less than 300 feet from the parking lot. While picnicking here, think about the 140 plus passengers on the trains marooned for three weeks in 1884 because of a blizzard. Many people almost starved—hence the name—but they were rescued by a group of skiers who came from Hood River. There are picnic tables near the base of the 180- plus-foot waterfall. Consider bringing bikes and spinning on the paved trail from Starvation Creek to Viento State Park. Public restrooms.

Getting There: From Hood River, drive west on I-84 for 11 miles and take Exit 51 (Wyeth). Double back on I-84 heading east until the well-marked Starvation Creek Exit 55.

Photo by Patrick Hiller

Ahhh!

Stratton Gardens

🅰️ *Hood River, OR*

This wonderful urban picnic spot has plenty of benches and lots of fragrant flowers. Located on Sherman St. between Horsefeathers Restaurant and the Courthouse. If you find yourself in the middle of town, hike up the stairs next to the fish fountain and enjoy this lovely garden. You'll find a stellar view of the river and signage for all the plants.

🧭 **Getting There:** Located between 2nd and 3rd Sts. and State and Sherman Sts. in downtown Hood River.

Photo by Maura Muhl

Lunching in style

Photo by Paloma Ayala • www.fotoisphoto.com

 Tucker Park
📍 *Hood River, OR*

Tucker Park is a popular camping area in the summer. In fact it was the first place we camped when we visited Hood River decades ago. Just before the entrance to the campground, you'll find plenty of picnic tables, a sink and a place to barbeque. You can picnic here or take the trail north of the picnic tables that leads to the south bank of the Hood River. Supplement your picnic with a huckleberry milkshake or cherry pie from the Apple Valley Country Store less than a mile away.

Getting There: From Hood River, head south on 13th St. which turns into Tucker Rd. Just after mile marker 5, stay right toward Dee and follow the signs to Tucker Park. (541) 386-4477 • www.co.hood-river.or.us

Photo by Jeff Faaborg

CHAPTER 8

EXCITING
Expeditions

Photo by Blaine Franger • www.blaineandbethany.com

The Gorge is famous for expeditions. The most famous one was led by Lewis and Clark who journeyed from Missouri to the Pacific Ocean. The explorers reached the Columbia River on October 16, 1805 and took their canoes on a treacherous journey down river. Perhaps you are not ready to traverse the entire country, but if you are looking for a longer outing, here are some ideas. What follows are adventures that require a little planning and may take a whole day. Figure out how much time you want to spend (and because kids are involved add another hour or so) and get going!

- Bike, Camp and Fish on the Deschutes River

- Board the Sternwheeler

- Find the Petroglyphs at Columbia Hills State Park

- Explore Bird Creek Meadows

- Investigate Mount St. Helens

- Search for a Geocache

- Go Spelunking Inside the Ice Caves

- Look up at the Stars

- Play along "Waterfall Alley" —Scenic Historic Columbia River Hwy.

- Ride the Mt. Hood Railroad

- Ski and Snowboard at Timberline

- Stay at The Flying L. Ranch and Explore Conboy Lake National Wildlife Refuge

- Zipline at Skamania

Bike, Camp and Fish on the Deschutes River

21 *Wasco, OR—near Rufus, OR*

1 *Easy* ◐ ✿ *Spring and Fall*

All loaded up

Once the site of the railroad wars of the early 1900's, the Deschutes River Canyon is often sunny when it's raining in the western gorge. The 32 mile round trip Old Railbed Trail on the east bank of the river winds up the canyon through sagebrush hills and past some of the premier fishing in the Pacific Northwest. When your family feels adventurous, pack the bikes, fishing rods and camping gear for overnight fun. Young kids can ride their bikes on the relatively flat trail or jump in the bike trailer when their legs tire of pedalling.

Take a break from biking, pull out the fishing rod and you'll have dinner in no time. Not that adventurous? Set up a tent at the campground at the mouth of the river and then hike on one of the trails. The four mile loop from the Blackberry to the Riverview Trail is fairly flat. Beware of the goat head thorns (they pop tires in seconds) and rattlesnakes. Make sure to bring a patch kit and extra tubes just in case. Primitive sites $6-$10/ night; $5 for overnight parking. 89600 Biggs-Rufus Hwy., Wasco • (541) 739-2322 • www.oregonstateparks.org

Cruising up the Gorge

Photo courtesy of Portland Spirit

Board the Sternwheeler

🧭 *Cascade Locks, OR*   ❶ *Easy*

☀️ ✿ 🌙 *Daily cruises from June to October, modified schedule in November and May.*

All Aboard! Take a boat ride on the Sternwheeler, an old-fashioned paddle wheel. The journey up and down the Columbia River begins at the docks in Cascade Locks and is an ideal outing with the grandparents. The ride lasts two hours, the perfect amount of time before anyone starts jumping overboard. During your cruise, the Captain tells the passengers about the geological formation of the river, the Lewis and Clark expedition and the construction of the Bonneville Dam in 1938. Our kids had fun exploring the boat and were especially keen on watching the paddle wheel go round-and-round and propel the boat. You can pack a picnic or dine on board—the food is good! Bring warm jackets even if you think you don't need them and make sure the Captain doesn't run over any of the sailboats, kiters or windsurfers! Tickets cost $28 per adult; $18 for kids (4-12); 3 and under are free.

🧭 **Getting There:** From Hood River, drive west on I-84 for 20 miles to Exit 44. Drive into Cascade Locks and turn right on Sternwheeler Dr. Follow the signs to the Marine Park. (503) 224-3900 • www.sternwheeler.com

Find the Petroglyphs at Columbia Hills State Park

📍 Just east of Dallesport, WA

① ② Easy to Moderate   ◐ ☀ ❀ April through September

When the Native Americans lived here, some created pictographs and petroglyphs on the rocks overlooking the river. Pictographs are rock paintings; petroglyphs are rock carvings. At that time, the lake didn't exist. When the Dalles Dam flooded the village it created the lake and submerged much of the rock art. Some of the petroglyphs were high enough to escape the flood and many were relocated to higher ground. The park has one of the most extensive collections of these rock paintings, the most famous named "Tsagaglalal" or "She Who Watches." When you stand underneath this painting, you'll feel her power. Both a petroglyph and a pictograph, She Who Watches is the largest and clearest painting in the Gorge. The parking area on the south side of the park has some rock art, but to see Tsagaglalal up close, make a reservation with the ranger station (509) 439-9032. Tours last more than one hour and occur Friday and Saturday mornings at 10:00 am.

At the campground, the ranger has treasure maps for children to identify the wooden bears, geese, squirrels and other animals hidden in the trees. We like fishing in the lake or paddling around on the SUP. For more adventure, head east to Horsethief Butte, a little more than one mile down the highway from the park. This is a prime place for serious rock climbers. We love to walk inside the butte and play around on the rocks.

Photos by Lisa Kosglow

Seaweed Mermaid

She who watches ▶

Explore Bird Creek Meadows

Mt Adams area, WA   **Easy to difficult**

Late August or September to avoid mosquitos, Spring for wildflowers

On the Yakima Nation Reservation, Bird Creek Meadows has lots of places to hike, camp and swim. We like to van camp at Bird Lake and then hike half a mile up to Bluff Lake where you can circumnavigate the sparkling lake and get a fabulous view of Mt. Adams. Bold ones may jump into the screaming cold but refreshing lake. One of the best kid-friendly hikes is the little more than one mile hike to Bird Creek Meadows and the Hellroaring viewpoint at the base of Mt. Adams. There's a creek and small waterfall providing lots of enjoyment. In the fall, feast on huckleberries and marvel at the wildflowers. Look out for grazing cows. The road through the reservation isn't for the family commuter car and is best with a 4-wheel drive and/or good clearance to navigate the rutted road. After the long drive (about 1.5 hours), we recommend staying the night. It's worth it!

Getting There: Cross the Hood River Bridge, turn left on Hwy. 14, then right on Hwy. 141A. Drive 20 miles to Trout Lake, and stay right onto Mt. Adams Road for 1.3 miles until the junction with FR 23 (also FR 82). Continue for about .5 mile. Make sure to stay right when you reach FR 80 and stay on FR 82. Continue on FR 82 for 8.3 miles past FR 80. Here, FR 82 becomes both the Bureau of Indian Affairs Road 285 and FR 8290. Continue for another 4.2 miles until Mirror Lake and the junction of BIA 304 which takes you to Bird Lake. The Bird Creek Meadows trailhead is another mile. Park on the left.

Photo by Blaine Franger • www.blaineandbethany.com

Conked out

Investigate Mt. Saint Helens

📍 *Gifford Pinchot National Forest, WA*

❄️ *Year round*

On May 18, 1980 at 8:32 am, Mt Saint Helens blew its top, drastically trans-forming creeks into lakes and ponds, burning the forests and spewing forth lava. During the nine hour eruption, a mushroom shaped cloud of volcanic ash and gas rose thousands of feet into the sky, and rained gray ash on eastern Washington and beyond.

Today, you can venture to the volcano for a family friendly hike, a backpacking excursion or an intense 21 mile bike ride across the Plains of Abraham. We rode up the volcano as a family and it took most of the day. It was the most dramatic ride. At times we felt like we could be pedalling on the moon. From the Gorge, you can access Mt. Saint Helens through Carson, Washington. It's about a 100 mile drive to the base. On your way to this south side entrance, stop and scramble through the Ape Cave lava tubes. The upper Ape Cave is 1.5 miles long and the lower cave is .75 miles. It's cold and damp down below, even in the summer so bring warm layers and closed toe shoes with good trac-tion. Don't forget a few headlamps too!

The west side entrance, the one closer to Portland, has a 50 mile road that takes you to the Johnston Ridge Observatory, well into the blast zone. Along the way, there are a number of places to stop, hike and learn about the geology

Summit push

Photos by Robin Dickenson

of the area. During the summer, the Forest Service interpreters lead a wide range of activities, from short walks to amphithe-ater presentations. In the winter, you can cross-country ski and snowmobile the trails.
(360) 274-7750 • www.fs.usda.gov
See also www.mshinstitute.org

Search for a Geocache

All over the world

Year round

Geocaching is one of the hottest high tech games of hide and seek where people search for hidden treasures with the assistance of a global positioning sys-
tem (GPS) device. The game was invented by fellow Oregonian, David Ulmer
on May 3, 2000, the day after the US Department of Defense enabled GPS
signals of 24 satellites to be more accurate, thus essentially opening the doors
for the public use of GPS units. Ulmer, a computer consultant in Portland, hid
a few treasures, posted their GPS coordinates on a newsgroup and eventually
launched, www.geocaching.com, which now has more than one million caches,
stashed in hundreds of places around the world.

Here in the Gorge, we have lots of caches, the technical word for containers.
You can log on to www.geocaching.com to find the most up-to-date GPS
latitude and longitude coordinates marking the hidden caches and then off
you go in search of the treasure, just like Captain Hook. Typically, if you take
something from the geocache, you need to replace it with something of equal
value. The treasures are usually small trinkets with little value such as coins,
cards, key chains and plastic animals. Don't forget to document your experience in the geocache logbook and put the cache back in its hidden place.
www.geocaching.com

Shane with ice in August

Go Spelunking Inside the Ice Caves

㉑ Guler, WA (West of Trout Lake)

❷ ❸ Moderate to difficult inside the ice caves

◐ ☀ ❀ Spring, summer or fall

Put on your warm clothes, sensible shoes, bike helmets and headlamps and venture to the Guler Ice Caves. These big lava tubes stay chilly enough to have ice in them all year round. In fact during the pioneer days before refrigerators existed, locals stocked their homes with ice from the caves.

Walking through the caves is challenging because the ground is a pile of ice, rocks and water and requires some bouldering. You can explore the mouth of the cave, or make your way inside and down the tubes. In the spring, you'll find tons of icicles and hear lots of dripping noises. Try turning your flashlights off in the middle and experience total darkness. The cave right next to the parking area is well marked with wooden steps leading you down under. For more caves, take the narrow path just across the parking lot. You can also walk inside these caves and see where you'll come out. Pit toilets and picnic area are located at the mouth of the cave. For more geological wonders, explore the Natural Bridges a little more than one mile away. These bridges formed when the flowing hot lava tubes cooled into caves, which over the years collapsed. The collapsed areas became trenches and the intact parts became bridges.

Getting There: Cross the Hood River Bridge, turn left on Hwy. 14, then right on Hwy. 141A. Drive 20 miles to Trout Lake, and bear left, past the Ranger Station. Drive 5.7 miles on FR 24 to the Ice Caves. To see the Natural Bridges, backtrack to FR 24, turn left for .8 mile, another left on FR 041 for .5 mile.

Look up at the Stars
🅠 *Goldendale, WA*

Visit the Goldendale Observatory where you can gaze at the sky through one of the nation's largest public telescopes, a 24.5 inch Cassegrain reflecting telescope and built in 1973 by four amateur astronomers. With this amplification, it seems possible to jump up and land on the moon. Make sure to have the onsite astronomer show you Saturn and its rings. Night viewings usually begin around 8:00 pm and include a short educational lecture about the stars. You can also observe the sun and it's sun spots in the afternoon. Mark your calendar- on August 21, 2017, we will have a full solar eclipse (that's when the moon's shadow touches the earth and the sun disappears for a few minutes during the day). Oregon will be a prime viewing place. Though there is no admission fee, you might be so wowed by our universe that it will inspire you to make a donation. Check the website for other upcoming celestial events.

Getting There: From Hood River, head east on I-84 for 40 miles to exit 104. Continue on US 97 through the town of Goldendale. Follow the signs. 1602 Observatory Dr. (509) 773-3141 • www.goldendaleobservatory.com

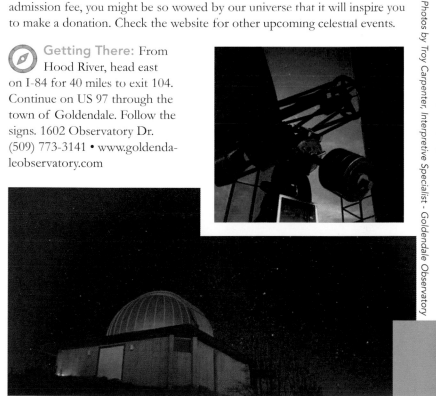

Photos by Troy Carpenter, Interpretive Specialist - Goldendale Observatory

Play along "Waterfall Alley"— Scenic Historic- Columbia River Hwy.

Ainsworth to Crown Point, OR

We've named this 12-mile gorgeous stretch of the Old Highway from Ainsworth to Crown Point "Waterfall Alley" because it has the highest concentration of waterfalls in the world. Along with the waterfalls, you'll find tons of hikes, places for picnics and streams for splashing and rock throwing. The trees and water keep the area cool, which can be especially desirable on our hot summer days. It's a must see for visitors, and depending on everyone's motivation, you may want to drive the section of the highway up to Crown Point or hike one of the numerous trails. The hike up Horsetail Falls to Ponytail Falls is short and impressive because it takes you behind the waterfall. Another short hike is to walk up the path to the Multnomah Falls' bridge, but we prefer to hike the long way from Wahkeena to Multnomah Falls. Venture to the remodelled Crown Point for a spectacular view of the Gorge. On windy days, it feels like you could fly all the way to Kansas. Inkling to splash in the water? Check out Oneonta Gorge. Go with the flow—just like the water flying from the falls.

>> *Selfie!*

Ride the Mt. Hood Railroad

Area: Hood River, OR

Season: June-October; December for Polar Express

All Aboard! Take the 4 hour round trip train excursion to Parkdale. The train winds through our fruit tree studded valley with glorious snowcapped mountain views visible along the way. Little ones will be thrilled to walk between the cars and gaze out the windows. Buy lunch on the train or stop in Parkdale for ice cream and BBQ or visit at the Hutson Museum before returning to town.

Another fun train experience happens in the winter when the Polar Express comes to town. During this popular trip, passengers wear PJ's and sip hot chocolate while Santa's elves read them the classic book, "The Polar Express." The bearded man himself is on board with special gifts for the kiddos. Shorter than the summer train ride, this train travels part way up the valley to the North Pole (Pine Grove) complete with decorations, lights and waving elves. Tickets can be spendy between $20 and $60 depending on dates, seating and age of ticket holder. We recommend saving this outing for an adventure with the grandparents.

Getting There: From downtown Hood River, turn left on 2nd St. and right on Cascade. Park near the train. 110 Railroad Ave. Hood River (800) 872-4661 www.mthoodrr.com

Photo courtesy of Mt. Hood Railroad

😀 Ski and Snowboard at Timberline

📍 Government Camp, OR

Snow in Summer

Photo by Lisa Kosglow

Built in 1929 during the Great Depression, Timberline Lodge is an intriguing place to explore year round and a great place to spend the night. After sipping on the best hot chocolate around, take a look at the exhibits about the history of the lodge and President Franklin Delano Roosevelt's projects to help America survive the Depression.

Timberline is the only place to ski and snowboard in the summer in the United States. A summer trip to the snow may reward you not only with an exciting ride down the hill, but also autograph opportunities with the best skiers and snowboarders in the country. Ride the Magic Mile chairlift with skis or a snowboard to the Palmer snowfield for some summer shredding of your own. Don't snowboard? No worries. Get a foot passenger ticket and ride to 7,000 ft for a snowball fight! Also during the summer and fall, you can hike right from the lodge. Try the 4.4 mile roundtrip hike to Zigzag Canyon and the short but steep 2.2 mile hike to Silcox Hut. In winter, you can ski, snowboard or cruise along their snowshoe trail. If you're around for Labor Day, come up for the

Photo by Paloma Ayala • www.fotoisphoto.com

family friendly Mountain Music Festival in the outdoor amphitheater. Cap your summer off with huckleberry shakes, dancing and stunning views of Jefferson, Three Sisters and Bachelor in the distance.

🧭 **Getting There:** From Hood River, drive 40 miles south on Hwy. 35 and veer right to Hwy. 26. until you see a sign for Timberline Lodge on the right. Turn right and follow the access road to the Wy'East day lodge. Park and walk uphill to the historic lodge. (503) 272-3311 • www.timberlinelodge.com

Stay at The Flying L Ranch and/or
Explore Conboy Lake National Wildlife Refuge
📍 *Glenwood, WA*

Looking for an easy overnight get-away? Located at the base of Mt. Adams, just 35 minutes north of Hood River, the Flying L Ranch has rustic rooms and cabins. Large groups can rent the main lodge with use of the kitchen and fireplace room. Prepare group meals, play monopoly and scrabble next to the roaring fire, sip hot chocolate and munch on popcorn. You get the picture. It's cozy! When there's enough snow, you can cross country ski from the back-door and in the summer, hike on trails right on the property.

If you want to explore the area, owners and adventurers Julee Wasserman and Tim Johnson can give you the scoop about Mt. Adams and Conboy Lake National Wildlife Refuge, only five miles away. Home to elk, coyotes, rabbits and tons of birds, the refuge is more of a marsh than a lake and attracts a number of migrating birds and animals all year round. In winter, look for tracks or spot coyotes hunting for a meal. In the spring and summer search for the rare Oregon spotted frog and the sandhill cranes. At the visitors center, you can walk through the historic Whitcomb-Cole Hewn Log House.

Getting There: Cross the Hood River Bridge, turn left on Hwy. 14, then right on Alt. Hwy. 141 and left on Hwy. 141. Drive 12 miles to BZ Corner, turn right on BZ Glenwood Hwy. and continue 19 miles to Glenwood. In town, another right and drive east for about 1/2 mile toward Goldendale. Make a left on Mt. Adams Hwy. In a 1/2 mile, turn into the driveway on the right.
25 Flying L Lane
(509) 364-3488
www.mt-adams.com
www.fws.gov

Photo courtesy of Flying L Ranch

Zipline at Skamania

 Stevenson, WA   ❄ **Year round**

Eager to fly through the trees like the Howler monkeys in Costa Rica? Head to Skamania and hook up to one of their 7 ziplines. Some of them are really long, like 900 feet where you are way up there with the eagles. Open most of the year, even in the rain which owner Shane compares the zipping to surfing in the rain. Our favorite is Saks Fifth Avenue where you funnel through the tall trees, hooting and hollering along the way. Kids need to be 60 pounds to zip. A bit expensive, but guaranteed to rush your adrenaline.

Getting There: Drive I-84 west to Cascade Locks, cross the Bridge of the Gods and turn left on Hwy. 14. Follow signs to Skamania Lodge. 1131 SW Skamania Lodge Way • (509) 427-0202 • zipnskamania.com

Photo courtesy of Skamania Lodge Zipline

Just Do It!

I dream big, but I also leave things to the last minute and am not a good planner. When my husband Tim and I married, we promised each other we would take our future children sailing, not just a short sail on the Bay, but on the ocean so they would become strong, capable, resilient kids. It was difficult to toss away the landlines, but in 2008, we fulfilled our marital promise. Our two children were old enough to swim safely on their own so we bought Kamaya, a Stevens 50, in May, and sailed under the Golden Gate Bridge five months later. We didn't give ourselves much time to fully prepare. Perhaps, if we had made the time, we might have listened to the sceptics who asked "who in their right mind would take a 7 and 8 year old on the ocean?" We had amazing experiences. We swam with dolphins, whales and manta rays. We lived in numerous countries, learned Spanish in Guatemala, studied the giant tortoise and Darwin in the Galapagos and tasted sea urchins and coconut crabs in the island of Suwarrow. I share this with you, not to encourage you to sail across the Pacific, but to urge you to seize the moment while you are here in the Gorge and to have exciting adventures with your kids. Time passes quickly and toddlers become teenagers rapidly. ~ Ruth

CHAPTER 9

EXTREME SPORTS
WITH *Kids*

Photo by Richard Hallman • www.freelanceimaging.com

Tucker hucking

120

Here in the Gorge we have more opportunities for outdoor excitement per square foot than any other place in the world. As a result, most of us are involved in some sort of sport or another, whether it's snowboarding, kiteboarding or windsurfing. Extreme? Well, just come try. Remember to pack your helmets, kneepads and sense of adventure!

- Climbing
- Fishing
- Horsebackriding
- Kiteboarding
- Windsurfing

- River Rafting/ Kayaking
- Sailing
- Skateboarding
- SUP'ing it Up

Climbing

We have fun opportunities for climbing, from the fabricated Life Rocks to the real deal at Horsethief Butte. This section isn't a replacement for a rock climbing guide but rather gives you a heads up to some of the family friendly places around the Gorge. Obviously, there are inherent risks in climbing as well as many of the activities described in our book, so please use common sense and climb on!

Climbing Cooper

Photo by Lisa Kosglow

121

Bulo Point
Mt. Hood, OR

The Forest Service Road 44 area hosts a slew of adventure possibilities. There are a number of campgrounds for extended trips, horseback riding, mountain biking, hiking and Bulo Point for climbers. The short approach, bolted and crack lead climbing and accessible top roping make this spot fun for all ages and suitable for beginners. Climbs are rated 5.6-5.10+ with at least 5 cracks to explore. There are some solid bouldering problems in the area as well. The FR 44 road is closed during the winter so ideal time to visit Bulo is mid-May through the end of October.

Getting There: Drive south from Hood River on Hwy. 35 for about 40 miles. Between Sherwood and Robin Hood campground turn east on FR 44. Drive another 10 miles, then turn on FR 4420 for about one mile, make a left on FR 4421 which leads to FR 240. Stay right, and continue for one mile until you see the trail on your left. Park and hike 2 minutes to the Crag.

Frenches Dome
Near ZigZag, OR on Mt. Hood

The remains of an old volcano, Frenches Dome is a 100 ft basalt formation deep in the woods on Mt Hood. A short approach, lots of holds and easy parking make it a great stop for families. Described as "sporty, crimpy and pumpy," Frenches Dome is a locals favorite crag for climbing with kids. Bolted, sport routes rate between 5.5 and 5.13 so kids and parents will both be challenged. Be aware of the steep hillside if you're towing young wee ones. There are campgrounds in the area.

Getting There: From Hood River, drive south on Hwy. 35 then take Hwy. 26 to Zig Zag. Turn right onto Lolo Pass Rd and continue for approximately 6 miles. The dome is not clearly visible from the road, but you'll see an obvious dirt pullout with parking on the right. Take the small trail downhill to the dome; the majority of the climbs are on the left side of the dome.

Horsethief Butte
📍 *Dallesport, WA*

For kids and families, one of our favorite climbing spots is Horsethief Butte where the cliffs aren't too intimidating and setting up top ropes is easy yet still exposed. Endless rock scrambling abounds. Kids love to climb and spot small lizards also scaling across the rocks. Poison oak is abundant so be aware and stay on the trail. Pit toilets are at the parking area. For a fantastic full day, complement the climbing with a visit to the petroglyphs at Columbia Hills State Park.

Photo by Lisa Kosglow

Climb on!

From Fear to Confidence

Many of us grew up with parents telling us to, "be careful," "watch out!" or not to do something because we could get hurt. They didn't want to take us to the emergency room plus they might have been scared themselves. However, sometimes when a well intentioned parent says, "be careful," his child may actually tense up and get scared. While training for snowboarding, I learned the power of changing my perspective. I learned to retrain the way I spoke to myself and tap into my strength and empowerment, instead of my fear. When I was first competing, I used to think, "look out for the tree or the huge rut at turn 5," but after working with a sports psychologist, I shifted my approach to "look to the next gate or take a wide line around turn 5." Now as a parent, I use this same technique with my daughter who loves to climb on everything. Instead of saying "be careful" when she's climbing a tree, I tell her to "pay attention" and give her specific feedback on where to put her feet and hands. She's gaining confidence and I'm being helpful and supportive. We'll see if I continue this approach when she wants to learn a Double Cork 1080 in the halfpipe. ~ Lisa

I can fly

Life Rocks Climbing
📍 Hood River, OR

Owner Keith Whigham, a big kid himself, has created a safe but fun environment for kids to play and test their climbing skills. Kids practice tricks on the two bungee trampolines with harnesses, burn off energy on the endless climbing tread wall, or don a velcro suit and bounce on the inflatable and huck themselves at the velcro wall. On hot summer days, Keith turns on the water and transforms the inflatable into a slip-and-slide. Young children can learn the alphabet and numbers the fun way—through climbing challenges. The smallest climbers (3-6 yrs) play on the climbing mountain. Open to all ages and available for birthday parties. Cost is $12 for a day pass with options for family and season passes. See website for dates and hours. Open April 1-Sept 30. 1109 13th St.
(805) 637-9633 • www.liferocksclimbing.com

Fishing

Fish on! Be warned -- you might hook a 10-foot sturgeon or even a 20-pound salmon! The Columbia River has one of the largest runs of salmon and steelhead outside of the great state of Alaska. The Oregon Department of Fish and Wildlife hosts a number of kids fishing days. Make sure to get a license for kids 14 years or older.

Deschutes River
📍 The Dalles to Warm Springs, OR

We have premier fishing in our own backyard! Anglers come from all over the world to fish the Deschutes River which starts in Warm Springs and meanders for more than 100 miles before meeting up with the Columbia River. Cast away!

Lost Lake
📍 *Dee, OR*

All boat rentals include life jackets, whistles, and oars or paddles. Even if you don't catch a fish, you can catch some sensational photos of Mt. Hood looming in the background. If you don't land a fish, look for salamanders swimming in the shallows.

Laurance Lake Reservoir
📍 *Parkdale, OR*

Located about 9 miles from Hood River, this reservoir is stocked with trout and open year round if you can maneuver through the winter snow. Here are the rules: you must tell jokes, eat greasy chips and talk about the big fish that got away!

Caught a big one!

Fishing Derbies

The Oregon and Washington Fish and Wildlife both host fishing derbies throughout the summer. A fun introduction to fishing, derbies, like the one in Trout Lake, show kids how in just 10 minutes, fish in a stream can become dinner on a plate. Volunteers are close by to help with the transformation by putting wiggly worms on hooks, unhooking wiggly fish from hooks, cleaning and gutting wiggly fish, and battering and frying non-wiggly fish in a pan. You get the idea. They assist in surmounting the challenging parts of fishing. For more info check out these websites. www.wdfw.wa.gov • www.dfw.state.or.us

Horsebackriding

The Gorge has incredible open spaces and idyllic ranches and trails for horses to gallop. Some horse enthusiasts join the Pony Club and compete, others want to hop on a horse and ride trails on other people's horses. Here are some equestrian opportunities.

Double Mountain Horse Ranch
Hood River, OR

This ranch offers a variety of horse adventures through the Hood River Valley, including simple trail rides to birthday parties. They also have a number of kids camps in the summer. 3995 Portland Dr.
(541) 513-1152 • www.ridinginhoodriver.com

Northwestern Lake Riding Stables
White Salmon, WA

Ride 'em cowboy! This riding stable in the Gorge offers a variety of trail rides for children 8 years and older. The one hour Creek trail ride through the lush green forest is ideal and exciting, especially in the spring when the river is high and the ferns and wildflowers decorate the path. They ride many other stellar trails and host a summer camp. 1262 Little Buck Creek Road
(509) 493-4965 • www.nwstables.com

Pony Club

For the keen equestrians, consider joining the Mt. Hood Pony Club. The club trains together, and travels to all sorts of competitions and equestrian events. Our local Pony Club has not only excelled in a number of competitions, but they are also a super organization for young equestrians to learn horse-care funda-

Photo by Sue Davis

mentals and sportsmanship. You don't need to own a horse to join! Find them on Facebook or take a look at www.oregonponyclub.org

Photo by Jim Greenleaf

Trotting through the blossoms

Kiteboarding

Kids as young as seven years old can learn to kiteboard, but most schools encourage waiting until they're at least nine and we think even older could be better depending on the child. Older kids whose frontal lobes might be more connected, might be apt to make safe decisions while on the water. Kiting, like many sports, can be dangerous, but it sure is fun to zoom across the river and fly through the air.

Cascade Kiteboarding
🅟1 Hood River Event Site

Local Pro, Tonia Farman runs a tight ship at Cascade Kiteboarding and has created an excellent learning environment. Instructors give private lessons with radio helmets and assist students on their jet ski. The staff offers kite clinics and kids camps for kids as young as nine years old. (541) 392-1212 www.cascadekiteboarding.com

Photo by Peter Foley

Zippin' through the river

Photo by Ruth Berkowitz

New Wind Kite School
🅟1 Hood River Kite Spit

They love the fact that kiting teaches so many life skills, including teamwork, persistence, independence and focus. Instructors follow students with a jet ski and a head set. (541) 387-2440 • www.kiteschool.com

The Gorge Kite School
🟤 Hood River Sand Bar

This school offers private lessons to anyone who weighs at least 70 pounds. Owner Mark Worth believes that kids with good judgment recognize the dangers of kiteboarding, and with proper instruction will learn how to be safe on the water. But he says kids also are some of his best students and learn incredibly fast. (541) 490-4401 • www.gorgekiteboardschool.com

River Rafting/Kayaking

Want to get wet and raft down one of our raging rivers? If your child can swim, and is ready to hop in a raft, here are a few local outfitters that will guide you down the river.

All Adventures in the Gorge: If you're 9 years old or older, this family-owned company will guide you down the wildest or mildest river. They guarantee that rafting will build teamwork and an appreciation of the wilderness. (800) 74-FLOAT (35628) • www.alladventures.com

River Rider: A river rider is someone who loves whitewater and wants other people to enjoy it as well. This group takes young kids whitewater rafting on Class I and II rivers. Hwy. 141 near Husum (800) 448-RAFT (7238) • www.riverrider.com

Little kid, big rapid

Photo by Lora Melkonian

Wet Planet Rafting: Wet Planet helps 9 year olds and older experience the raging rapids and the calm smooth waters of the White Salmon, Wind River and Klickitat. They also host a summer kayak camp where kids practice rolls in their pool and learn how to read the river.
(800) 306-1673 • www.wetplanetwhitewater.com

World Class Kayak Academy: Have an adventurous high schooler who wants to kayak and go to school at the same time? Based right in our backyard in Trout Lake, the Academy takes students far beyond the Northwest and into remote cultures and rivers all over the world, including Chile, Canada and China. Students study in the morning and kayak in the afternoon.
(541) 908-5937 • www.worldclassacadamy.com

Zoller's Outdoor Odysseys, Inc.: Enthusiastic and competent kids as young as 6 can paddle and float down the White Salmon and Klickitat Rivers. With the removal of Condit Dam, Zollers offers three distinct sections to run on the White Salmon. Owner Mark Zoller used to work with UPS, so he runs a tight ship, one that's organized and on time. Their facility has lots of toys, including a lounging BBQ area, volleyball courts, deli and a view.
(800) 366-2004 • www.zooraft.com

Perfect breeze

Sailing

Our sailing programs grow every year, providing numerous opportunities for young sailors. We have a number of professional sailors living in the Gorge, like Morgan Larson and Sean "Doogie" Couvreux. Many of these pros help coach young sailors. Kass and Lars Bergstrom recently started a high school sailing team. Learning to sail with heaps of wind is not only exciting, but also builds grit, character and talent.

GORGE Junior Sailing
Hood River, OR

Thanks to Jaime and Andy Mack, we have a thriving community sailing program in Hood River. Beginners learn the basics on seven foot long Optimist Sailboats and then upgrade to the two person 420s. Kids sail in circles around buoys or if they prefer forwards and backwards and sometimes sideways or upside down, given the strong winds. Watch out for the boom – there's a reason why it earned the name. Classes are held during the summer when the west wind blows and the water is warm. During July and August, Monday nights are open sailing nights, where parents and children sail in the marina.

Getting There: Take Exit 64 and turn left at the stop sign and continue on E. Port Marina Drive. The Sailing School practices right behind the DMV. Sign up through Hood River Community Education:
(541) 386-2055 • www.hrcommunityed.org

Columbia Gorge Racing Association
🅿️ *Cascade Locks*

One of the premier places to race dinghies (small boats), Cascade Locks can be calmer than other parts of the Gorge. Plus here the river is wider, so you don't have to tack constantly. The CGRA (Columbia Gorge Racing Association) hosts many world class regattas and offers sailing classes and clinics for kids. Take a look at their website for the latest programs, www.cgra.com

🧭 **Getting There:** Drive 20 miles west on I-84 to Exit 44, Cascade Locks. Turn right to the Marine Park and follow the road to the boats. www.cgra.com

Skateboarding

If your kids have graduated from the swings and are now rolling on skateboards, let them loose at one of these skateparks. It's amazing to watch the skaters snake around the ramps. If it's your child, maybe you better close your eyes!

Bingen Skatepark
🅿️ *Bingen, WA*

Located next to Daubenspeck Park (see Chapter 1, Monkeying Around the Playground) and built in 2011, this 6,000 sq ft. park features banks, rails a concrete pool and lots of smooth concrete for little shredders. A big shade tree in the middle of the park provides some shelter from the sun. The big kids come out after school and on weekends so if you have really little ones go when the older kids are in school.

🧭 **Getting There:** Cross the Hood River Bridge, turn right onto Hwy. 14. Drive one mile and turn left on Willow St. Follow the sign for "City Park." City of Bingen • (509) 493-2122

Hood River Rotary Skatepark

🏴 *Hood River, OR*

Constructed underneath the towering ponderosa pine trees, this impressive and shady skatepark has numerous rails and two large concrete bowls. There is also a covered area perfect for drizzly days. Weekday mornings are recommended for toddlers on balance bikes or skateboards, while any time works well for older kids on skateboards. There is a bathroom, picnic tables, a climbing structure and a stream for mucking around. With parental help, young kids on balance bikes or older kids on BMX or mountain

Sean ripping the bowl

bikes can try the dirt track on the hill above the skatepark. Thanks to the folks who worked hard to construct this park, it's now one of the best skateparks in Oregon!

 Getting There: From downtown, head west on Cascade Ave. turn right on 20th St., then left on Wasco St.
(541) 386-5720 • www.hoodriverparksandrec.org

The Dalles Skatepark - Thompson Park

🏴 *The Dalles, OR*

This skatepark is a happening place and particularly exciting since it is next to the brand new swimming pool (and Fun Jumpers.) Lots of transitions, rails and banks keep skaters, scooters and bikers zipping around. The sun can be intense during the summer, but rumor has it there are plans to install shade protection.

 Getting There: From Hood River, drive 20 miles east on I-84. Take exit 84, and merge onto W. 2nd St. until you reach the park.
602 W. 2nd St., The Dalles • www.nprd.org

Windells

🔟 Welches, OR

Snowboarders, freeskiers, skaters and BMX riders have one of the premier facilities in the country in our backyard. With 50,500 sq. ft of outdoor skate space and an indoor park with a foam pit for learning new tricks, Windells is a year-round paradise for all things action sports. Skateboarders, BMX riders, scooters and in-line skaters can drop in for open skate on Saturdays and Sundays during fall and winter months. They also host overnight week-long summer camps for snowboarders, freeskiers, skateboarders and BMX riders and a full-time accredited academy is available for high schoolers serious about pursuing these sports.

Getting There: An hour or 64 mile trip. Head south on Hwy. 35 and continue on Hwy. 26 until you reach Windells on the left side. 59550 E. Hwy. 26 Sandy • (503) 622-3736 • www.windells.com

SUPing It Up

Turn hot, windless days into adventure days! Stand up paddling or SUPing is one of the fastest growing water sports. The Gorge boasts a number of paddling areas for parents paddling with kids as passengers and young paddlers learning to paddle their own board. Rent gear from one of the various rental companies or bring your own and SUP it up!

Photo by Peter Foley

Sunset SUP

Horsethief Lake

🅰 *Columbia Hills State Park*
① *Easy*

When summer crowds swarm the beaches around Hood River, head east to Horsethief Lake. An expansive grassy area with plenty of mature shade trees borders the lake which is actually an inlet of the Columbia. Somewhat protected from west wind, the lake provides easy access for SUPing, swimming, fishing and other water play. Ample parking, public bathrooms, picnic tables with grills and a campground with a teepee make this spot an easy day trip or quick overnight. If you want to combine water play with a hike and rock scramble, hike to Horsethief Butte and make sure to check out the petroglyphs and pictographs.

Getting There: From Hood River, drive 20 miles east on I 84 until The Dalles. Take Exit 87 north and cross the bridge to Washington. Turn right on Hwy. 14 and proceed for one mile. You'll see signs for the park. Discover Pass required. www.parks.wa.gov

Life jacket? Check.

SUP Safety

• Oregon law requires adults to carry, and children ages 12 and under to wear, PFD's. In addition, all SUPers must have whistles.

• Consider the wind and wind forecast. Use judgment when deciding to go out. Getting blown downwind can be scary. For new paddlers, wind can make a fun activity miserable.

• Consider your child's comfort level before heading out with them. If she is scared, don't insist. Give her time to get used to the board by playing in shallow water. Work your way up to getting them to sit on the board for a ride.

Nichols Boat Basin

📍 Hood River, OR
① Easy

Kids are ready to go

With the increased popularity of SUPs, the Nichols Boat Basin is a happening place on windless hot summer afternoons. Formerly a working boat works with toxic substances that accompanies most shipyards, it now houses kayak and SUP outfitters as well as a few eating establishments on the dock. Park in the gravel parking lot just east of the Event Site where kids can pick blackberries while you unload gear. Somewhat protected from wind you can paddle around the boat basin or if you're feeling brave, head out into the Columbia on still days. Resist the urge to park little ones on the sand bar. It can be dangerous when kiters are launching and landing their kites, plus the sediment in the Nichols Basin may not be suitable for kids to play in because of past industrial use.

If you need gear you can rent from any of the outfitters at the Event Site or park at the Gorge Paddling Center parking area between the Event Site and the gas station. Gorge Paddling Center has lots of toys, including SUPs, one person kayaks for kids 8 years and older, and tandem kayaks for parents and younger kids. They provide lessons as well.

⊘ Getting There: From town, head north on 2nd St. over the Interstate towards the river front. Turn right on Riverside Dr. and left on N 1st St. Look for the gravel parking lot next to the water on the right. (541) 806-4190 • www.gorgekayaker.com

Rowena—Mayer State Park, OR

📍 Rowena, OR
① ③ Easy to Difficult

Rowena's Mayer State Park is a prime spot to SUP. You can launch at the park on the west end and paddle around the calm, relatively enclosed area, even pick blackberries from your board or venture into the wider section of the river. On a calm day, we like to SUP across the Columbia River and paddle up the Klickitat River. SUPing under the bridge is exciting. Look up under the bridge and you might see swallow nests. In the fall, look down and search for salmon swimming in the crystal clear water. Be careful about crossing the river. Watch out for barges and quick changes in the wind.

 Getting There: Take I-84 east to Rowena, Exit 76. Turn left and cross the Railroad Tracks continuing into the park.

Wells Island
Hood River, OR   **②** **Moderate**

Just west of The Hook in Hood River is a sandy, vegetated island that provides a perfect venue for young explorers. Park at the west end of The Hook and launch your SUP from the newly built launch or from The Hook, which is more protected. Paddle over to Wells island, circumnavigate it, or land on one of the sandy beaches and explore the paths. A favorite spot is the beach on the western side of the island. Ample driftwood for building forts and shallow water for wading and splashing. Bring a picnic and your imagination and young pirates or castaways can pass hours playing while mom and dad take turns going out for longer paddles.

Scouting the passage

Photo by Blaine Franger • www.blaineandbethany.com

 Getting There: From downtown Hood River, head north on 2nd Street and cross I-84. Drive straight at the four-way stop and at the next stop sign turn left on Portway. Drive to where the road turns to gravel. You are now on The Hook. Head to the west end of the hook and park.

Big Winds SUP Team:

During the summer, keen SUP'ers ages 10 to 17, can join the Big Winds Junior SUP Race Team. Practice starts early, 6:30 am, two or four times a week. Steve Gates and his coaches teach kids various paddle techniques, skill building and race tactics. While no experience is necessary, SUP'ers must be strong swimmers and fearless in rough waters. The program culminates the third week of August with the Gorge Paddle Challenge.
(541) 386-6086 • www.bigwinds.com

Race to next buoy

Windsurfing

The smaller and lighter rigs combined with the wide boards have made it much easier for kids to learn to windsurf. Steve Gates, owner of Big Winds and former Mayor of Hood River, says that many parents make the mistake of putting their kids on their own gear which is heavier and harder to maneuver. Another recipe for disaster is to teach kids on the days when experts are sailing on 3.0 sails. It's worth waiting for the right conditions and important to keep the windsurfing experience fun. There are a number of sailing schools in town with most lessons being offered at The Hook or the Hood River Marina.

Big Winds
🅜 *Hood River Event Site and The Hook, OR*

Big Winds offers a large selection of high performance kite, windsurf and SUP gear and the staff has a wealth knowledge. They have kid's windsurfing camps, rentals and lessons from their shop and The Hook.
207 Front St., Hood River • (541) 386-6086 • www.bigwinds.com

Dogs love it too...

Photo by Ruth Berkowitz

Gorge Groms: If you are in the Gorge for an extended period, consider joining the Gorge Groms windsurfing club. Not only a great way for kids to learn how to windsurf, Gorge Groms enables kids to try the sport without having their parents invest in equipment. Part of the Columbia Gorge Windsurfing Association (CGWA), the club has a storage container at The Hook filled with gear and sails that are rigged and ready for use. The group hosts clinics and helps make the sport fun and easy. Cost is $100 per family for the season. www.gorgewindsurfing.org

This is how you do it

Hood River Waterplay: Hood River Waterplay teaches kids who weigh at least 60 pounds. Students must also be able to swim a minimum of 20 feet before they can start sailing on the water. Lessons take place at Waterplay's private beach near the Marina, just behind the Hood River Inn. 541-386-WIND (9463) • www.hoodriverwaterplay.com

Windsurfing Classes through Community Education:
Both community education departments in Hood River and The Dalles offer windsurfing classes at a very reasonable cost.
(541) 386-2055 • www.hrcommunityed.org
(541) 296-6182 • www.cgcc.cc.or.us

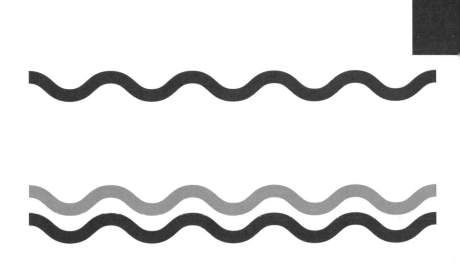

Water Quality

Unfortunately, we have to be concerned about the quality of water in the Columbia River. Coal dust, leaking nuclear waste upriver from Hanford, and agricultural run-off have contaminated our river, creating serious concerns about the safety of swimming. Most of us swim anyway, but if you want to dig deeper and assess the health risks for your family you can search the internet for assessments of the Columbia. Our local advocacy group, Columbia Riverkeeper, www.columbiariverkeeper.org, regularly tests the water quality at many of our beaches for E.coli and more. They have a number of suggestions to keep you safe, including rinsing off after swimming in the river, and swimming at least 500 feet upstream of any pipes discharging into the water. Take a look at their website and download their free Swim Guide app, www.theswimguide.org, for reports on water quality in the Gorge and beyond.

CHAPTER 10

Winter Fun

Snow day!

Sean getting rad at Meadows

Winter in the Gorge means skiing, sledding, snowboarding, snowshoeing and even ice skating. Put on your warm mittens and head outside. You'll find that we live in a winter paradise, and playing up at Mt. Hood is the best way to escape the cloudiness that often lingers around town. When its gray in town, you may find blue skies up at the mountain.

- Downhill Skiing and Snowboarding
- Cross Country Skiing
- Ice Skating
- Sledding and Tubing

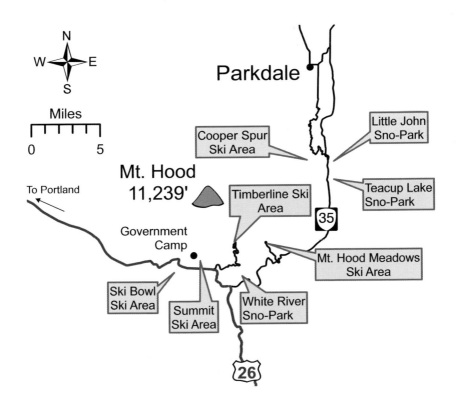

Downhill Skiing and Snowboarding

Outside Magazine once ranked Hood River as one of the top ten ski towns. Even though we seldom get snow in town, our mountains do. The skiing is challenging—just ask the National Ski team who trains on Mt. Hood during the summer. We have five downhill ski areas to choose from with Mt. Hood Meadows and Cooper Spur being the closest ones to Hood River. All offer rentals and lessons for kids and the price of admission pales to ski resorts in many other towns.

Cooper Spur Mountain Resort
📍 Mt. Hood, OR

This classic family ski area is the closest to Hood River—about 26 miles away. It is also one of the most affordable ski areas in the state and has one of the best ski teams around. If you've had enough of your skis, try tubing.

🧭 **Getting There:** Drive 23 miles south on Hwy. 35 and turn right at Cooper Spur Rd. Drive 2.5 miles to the Inn.
(541) 352-7803 • www.cooperspur.com

Mini shred

Photo by Melanie McCloskey

😃 Mt. Hood Meadows
📍 Mt. Hood, OR

Meadows' "fun zone" is the perfect place for beginners. Kids ride the magic carpet (like an escalator) up the hill. Not too far away, try Buttercup, a gentle beginner lift and in no time your young skier will be dragging you into Heather Canyon. When your kids peeter out, take them to the on-site daycare or enroll them in ski school. Snowboard lessons start at 4 years old. To jump start your kids progression, consider the three day Christmas camp or Spring Break camp.

Meadows also offers a variety of learn to ski and snowboard programs for kids ages 3 and older, including a Girls Camp and Freeride Team.

Getting There: Drive 36 miles south on Hwy. 35 until you see signs for Mt. Hood Meadows. There are two options: the lower HRM parking lot or the upper lot which is closest to the lodge and Fun Zone. (503) 337-2222 • www.skihood.com

Mt. Hood Ski Bowl
Government Camp, OR

Ski Bowl offers the most terrain for night skiing in America—with 34 lighted runs and a lighted terrain park and halfpipe. In the winter, they have a luge set-up, and in the summer there's an action park with bungee jumps, indy carts and mountain biking. Ski Bowl's longest run is three miles long. Wow!

Getting There: Drive 38 miles south on Hwy. 35 until you reach Hwy. 26 toward Portland. Ski Bowl is past Timberline. (503) 222-2695 • www.skibowl.com

Summit Ski Area
Government Camp, OR

The oldest ski area in the Northwest, Summit skiers started making turns down the slopes in 1927. It is open on weekends, and has an inner tube hill, a gentle lift and groomed cross-country trails. For the non-skiing parent, the lodge is perfectly situated such that you can read your book and watch your kids master the ski hill.

Getting There: Drive 38 miles south on Hwy. 35 and follow Hwy. 26 toward Portland. Continue 2.5 miles and turn right into Government Camp. The resort is in front of you when you turn off the highway. (503) 272-0256 • www.summitskiarea.com

Snowy romp

🙂 Timberline Lodge Ski Area
📍 *Mt. Hood, OR*

Skiing in the summer? That's right! It's winter all year round at Timberline. Timberline is also the only resort on Mt. Hood where you can stay slopeside. Enjoy their outdoor heated pool after skiing and wake up the next morning for some more runs. Built in 1933, the lodge was constructed during The Depression as part of the Works Progress Administration. It is now listed on the National Register of Historic Places and you'll see why when you visit. There's a huge fireplace, a number of restaurants and several exhibits about the construction of the lodge. During the summer, you can ski and snowboard with the national ski team and pro skiers and snowboarders from around the world. For the serious skier and snowboarder in your family, check out the summer ski and snowboard camps.

Cross Country Skiing

For those wanting to avoid the crowds of a downhill ski resort, cross country skiing may be your answer. We've had a host of memorable days out in the wild. Below are some of the groomed areas.

Mt. Hood Meadows
📍 *Mt. Hood, OR*

The Nordic Center located at Mt. Hood Meadows' lower lot, has 15 kilometers of groomed trails plus a hut to stow gear, wax skis and warm up with hot chocolate. You can rent skis and take lessons. A favorite trail is up to Sahalie Falls.

Cooper Spur Mountain Resort
Mt. Hood, OR

This area has 6.5 kilometers of groomed trails. When the sun is out and the snow just right, you can ski with a beautiful view of the mountain and enjoy lunch at the Resort or maybe even stay the night. Don't forget your sunscreen. Ski and snowshoe rentals are available at the lodge. 10755 Cooper Spur Rd • (541) 352-6692 • www.cooperspur.com

Mt. Adams Recreation Area
Trout Lake and Stevenson, WA

Washington's Gifford Pinchot National Forest divides into five areas, with Mt. Adams and Wind River being the closest. The Forest Service grooms miles of trails north of Trout Lake and in the Wind River area, near the town of Stevenson. Locals love the Old Man Pass Area with 32 miles of trails. The grooming of trails is done rather infrequently. Peruse the website for detailed information. (360) 891-5001 • www.fs.fed.us/gpnf

Teacup Lake Nordic
Mt. Hood, OR

Teacup has 12 miles of groomed trails for both skating and classic skiing. The heated wooden cabin is ideal to warm up, drink some hot chocolate (bring your own, there are no concessions at the warming hut) and tell stories about your Norwegian ancestors. Teacup is volunteer run and operates on donations only so please remember to come with cash. Cost is $10 suggested minimum donation for skiers 13 and over, 6-12 year olds are $5, 6 and under ski free. Family membership is $100 for the season.

Photo by Ruth Berkowitz

Looking good Ella!

Kick and glide

Trout Lake High School
📍 **Trout Lake, OR**

When conditions are right, the Trout Lake High School has a groomed track thanks to the generosity of the farm behind the school. The big wide open space and flat terrain sets the scene for an easy and tame family outing.

Getting There: Cross the Hood River bridge, turn left on Hwy. 14, right on Hwy. 141 Alt. until it merges with Hwy. 141. Turn left and continue for 19 miles until you reach the Trout Lake School on the right. 2310 Hwy. 141, Trout Lake • (509) 395-2571 • www.troutlake.k12.wa.us

Trillium Lake Basin
📍 **Government Camp, OR**

Located a few miles from Government Camp, the Trillium Lake area has 4.5 miles of classic groomed trails with stellar views of Mt. Hood. For a fun family outing, consider renting one of the cabins or homes and depending on the snow, you might have to ski in, so pack light.

Getting There: Drive 39 miles on Hwy. 35 until the turn off for Trillium Lake on the left side. It's before Government Camp.

Lovely day on the trail

Non-groomed trails

To take dogs and avoid a lift ticket, consider venturing to Bennett Pass right across from Mt. Hood Meadows or Pocket Creek, 34.5 miles south of Hood River. Both trails are a little off the beaten path and fun for all. Another great adventure is to ski up the Tilly Jane and Cooper Spur Trail.

Ice Skating

Perhaps someday we'll have an ice skating rink in the Gorge, but in the meantime if its cold and dry enough, there are a few natural places that ice up. Make sure the ice is safe and thick before exploring. The overflow mud puddle outside the Hood River Expo Center sometimes freezes and that's a great place to begin. The Bingen Marina has some spots that ice up. We've had some magical days up at Laurance Lake in Parkdale where folks play hockey and you can skate around the whole lake. If you're looking for a rink, here are three ice skating rinks near the Gorge:

Game on

Photo by Ruth Berkowitz

Mt. View Ice Skating Rink: 14313 SE Mill Plain Blvd., Vancouver, WA (360) 896-8700 • www.mtviewice.com

Lloyd Center Ice Rink: The rink can be crowded, but you can shop in the mall and do the Hokey Pokey at the same time.
953 Lloyd Center, Portland • (503) 288-6073 • www.lloydcenterice.com

Winterhawks Skating Center: 9250 Beaverton Hillsdale Hwy. (503) 297-2521 • www.winterhawksskatingcenter.com

Hang on!

Sledding and Tubing

Cooper Spur Mountain Resort
Mt. Hood, OR

This family resort has two tubing runs; the lower and the extreme! You must be at least 42 inches tall to tube down the mountain. Cost is $12 for an all-day ticket. (541) 352-6692 • www.cooperspur.com

Mt. Hood Ski Bowl
🔵 *Government Camp, OR*

Skibowl offers tubing and extreme tubing (yikes!), in the winter. The easier tubing hill is very wide and not too steep so your kids won't get scared. They also have an indoor super play zone for children to crawl, bounce, climb and slide.

Little John Sno-Park
🔵 *Mt. Hood, OR*

This Sno-Park has four sledding paths and when there's snow, sleds of all shapes and sizes whiz down the hill. The BIGGEST hill is 600 feet long—that's a long way to climb up and zoom down. Steel-runner sleds are prohibited. Little John is well equipped with pit toilets and an outdoor warming hut with a wood burning stove (bring your own wood). If you want to hike or cross country ski, try the trail on the left side of the park. Snowmobiles like the trail as well so it may be a little noisy.

Summit Ski Area
🔵 *Government Camp, OR*

During the weekend, you can tube down the hills. Summit has two sledding areas: one at the resort and another hill called Snow Bunny that is located 1 ½ miles east of the Timberline Junction on Hwy. 26.

😊 White River West Sno-Park
🔵 *Mt. Hood, OR*

This is a popular sledding hill, especially amongst Portlanders since it's closer to the city. The sledding paths are exhilarating. It's about a mile walk to the hill, but worth it! Whooping down the hill on a tube can be an enormous rush. Although our kids can tube forever, we leave when their clothes are soaked.

CHAPTER 11

WINDSURFING/KITING
Spots
FOR YOU AND YOUR
Tots

Anyone else want on?

Photo by Blaine Franger • www.blaineandbethany.com

Looking for the wind forecast?

To obtain daily conditions and forecasts, take a look at www.thegor-geismygym.com, www.iwindsurf.com and www.nwkite.com. Temira from The Gorge is my Gym, usually offers a weather forecast in the morning at 105.5 fm.

Windsurfing and Kiting can be a great family outing. The key to success is to pick a spot where parents can recreate while their tots enjoy the shore and stay away from the launch zone. We've also added kiting spots, but be sure kids play safely upwind of kite launch areas.

- Doug's Beach and the Lyle Sandbar
- The Hatchery
- Home Valley
- Hood River Event Site
- Hood River Marina
- Maryhill State Park
- Roosevelt Park
- Rowena
- Stevenson

Doug's Beach and the Lyle Sandbar
🅐 *Lyle, WA*

One of the premier windsurfing sites named after an expert windsurfer and owner of Doug's Sports, Doug's Beach is a fun place for kids and windsurfers. There are a few picnic tables and porta potties. Parking is at Hwy. 14's milepost 79 and you have to cross the railroad tracks to get to the beach, so please be cautious of trains.

Many beginner and intermediate kiters launch at the Lyle Sandbar because it's a huge beach, shallow and not as crowded as other places. However, the tree stumps in the water can be hazardous and sometimes the wind is gustier here. The sandbar has lots of fun places for kids to play. Consider complementing the kiting with a trip to Fischer Bridge to see the salmon swimming upstream in the fall.

🧭 **Getting There:** From Hood River, cross the bridge, turn right on Hwy. 14. Lyle is 10.8 miles on Hwy. 14. Doug's Beach is 15 miles on Hwy. 14. Discover Pass required.

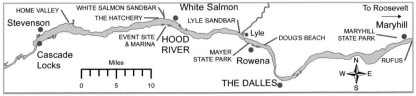

Map created by Matt Schrankel

The Hatchery and the White Salmon Sandbar
White Salmon, WA

The Hatchery is The—with a boldface capital "T"—place for expert windsurfers to show off their loops and flips. The swell can be gigantic and the wind fierce. It's an exciting place. Kids like to tuck into the woods and play along the shore where there is some wind protection and buckets of blackberries. You can also ride bikes to the fish hatchery and learn about our salmon. Parking $3/day or $50 summer pass. Some kiters use the challenging and rocky launch here, but most prefer to head east to the new beach by the White Salmon Bridge. Created recently, this sandbar resulted from the removal of the Condit Dam. It's a little tricky to access the beach and requires parking on the busy highway, but once you're down on the beach, there are lots of stick forts to construct.

Getting There: Cross the Hood River Bridge, turn left on Hwy. 14 for 5.1 miles. Turn left at Spring Creek Hatchery Rd.

Home Valley
6 miles east of Stevenson, WA

This sailing spot and campground has a protected beach that is shallow and exciting for kids. There's also a baseball diamond and buckets of blackberries in the summer. For the windsurfer and kiter, the grassy area makes rigging easier and you can sail here when the wind is blowing from the east or the west. No parking fee or permit required for day use, but there is a camping fee.

Getting There: Cross the Hood River Bridge, turn left on Hwy. 14 for 17 miles until the entrance to Home Valley Park. Cross the railroad tracks and the second right to the windsurfing area. (509) 427-3980, www.skamaniacounty.org

Hood River Event Site and Sandbar
🚩 *Hood River, OR*

This is one of the closest beaches to Hood River and usually has the most kids around as well. Windsurfers sail right off the beach and kiters pump up their kites on the east end of the Event Site and make their way across to the sand bar to launch their kites. You'll be happy with the huge lawn, restrooms, picnic tables, bleacher seats and large parking lot. Your kids will enjoy throwing rocks into the water here or they can play at the playground or swim at the Waterfront Park. Be wary of loads of windsurfing gear and windsurfers and kiters maneuvering their equipment. Parking costs $5/day or $50 summer pass.

Getting There: Drive north on 2nd St. and take the overpass across the freeway. Veer right on Portway Avenue. Parking fee for the entrance to the Event Site.

Photo by Robin Dickenson

Hood River Marina
🚩 *Hood River, OR*

Many beginner and intermediate windsurfers sail at the Marina because the shallow areas make it optimum for mastering water starts. It's also ideal for kids who can happily build sand castles or wade in the shallow water. Beware of the strong current in the middle. You can seek shelter from the wind on the west side of the beach or in the grassy area behind the beach. You'll find an even more protected lawn with trees just across the narrow parking lot. To add a little culture to your outing, walk to the Hood River Museum south of the beach. Parking is free.

Getting There: Make a left at the 4-way intersection of Hwy. 35 and head south to the Hood River Bridge. Make a left before the bridge and continue on E. Port Marina Dr. past the museum towards the river. (541) 386-1645, www.portofhoodriver.com

Maryhill State Park
📍 *Goldendale, WA*

This challenging windsurfing (it's not a great kiting spot) is ideal for kids. It has a roped off swimming area, a big grassy lawn, biking paths, restrooms, showers and comfortable camping. The beach contains big smooth stones, perfect for skipping rocks. If you want to detour from the beach, you can walk down the road to get peaches or hike up to the Stonehenge replica built by entrepreneur Sam Hill as a memorial to the soldiers from Klickitat County who died in World War I. For the windsurfer, be aware! The bridge makes it tough to see barges. The current can be strong. Parking $5/day or buy a Washington State Park pass for $50.

🧭 **Getting There:** Take I-84 east 40 miles to Exit 104, Yakima/Bend. Cross the bridge and drive one mile north on Hwy. 97. Take the first right, following signs to the Park. (509) 773-5007, www.parks.wa.gov

Roosevelt Park
📍 *Roosevelt, WA*

Located about one and a half hours east of Hood River, Roosevelt is an ideal place to camp out and sail or kite. Make sure to check the wind report before heading out. There's a big lawn, shady areas, restrooms, camping facilities and even a swing set. On your way, pick up some Maryhill peaches and pack food because there are few amenities nearby. Parking is free, but the lot fills up quickly.

Play time on the river

Photo by Ruth Berkowitz

🧭 **Getting There:** Take I-84 east 40 miles to Exit 104, Yakima/Bend. Turn right on Hwy. 14 for 34.4 miles until Roosevelt Park near milepost 133.

Rowena—Mayer State Park
🅐 *Rowena, OR*

This is another popular spot for families and rightly so because it usually has good wind and lots of places to explore. You'll find restrooms, picnic tables, a large rocky beach and areas that are protected from the wind. Our kids like to hang out around the trees, but it's also fun to play on the volcanic rock away from the windsurfers. Parking is $3 for the day, or $25 for a State Park season pass.

🧭 **Getting There:** From Hood River, drive east on I-84 for 12 miles to Rowena. Take Exit 76, go under the freeway across the railroad tracks and turn right until the end of the road. (800) 551-6949, www.oregonstateparks.org

Rufus
🅐 *Rufus, OR*

If your kids like rocks and the wind is right, this could be the place for you to kite while the rest of the family plays. Rocky Rufus can be less crowded than the kite beaches around Hood River. East of the launch is a small sandy cove where kids can play and throw rocks in the water. Warning—there have been some severe kitemares, causing injury to innocent bystanders and threatening the closure of Rufus. So long as the kiters launch on the river side of the beach, then kids are safe swimming in the cove. There are endless opportunities for rock throwing, rock stacking, rock rolling-you get the picture. Just keep the kids out of the launch zone! And no throwing rocks at the kites! Want to camp? Pitch a tent—up to 14 days for free.

🧭 **Getting There:** Cross the Hood River Bridge, turn left on Hwy. 14 for 20 miles until Stevenson. Take a left at any street in the middle of town and cross the railroad tracks.

Stevenson—Bob's Beach and East Point Kite Beach

📍 Stevenson, WA

Stevenson offers stellar kiting and windsurfing and is also a good place to go on east wind days. For windsurfing, Bob's Beach is family-friendly. The regulars even have their own facebook page and offer free wi-fi. Bob's Beach has a sloping lawn with plenty of trees for shade and protection from the wind. Other amenities include a changing cabana, and clean restrooms near-by. From the lawn, you can easily watch the sailors tacking and jibing. Kids love to throw rocks from the protected beach. If you are tired of sailing and hanging out, stroll along the waterfront or walk into town. Parking is free, but the lot can fill up fast.

Kiters recreate at the East Point Kite Beach, a third of a mile east near the boat ramp and beach. This is good site for kiting parents to take turns kiting while the kids ride bikes or skateboards away from the kite launch area on the paved trail to the west.

Getting There: Take Exit 44, Cascade Locks, and cross the Bridge of the Gods. Turn right on Hwy. 14 and continue 3 miles to Stevenson until the fork, bear right onto 1st St. (mile marker 14). At the stop sign, another right on Russell St., cross the railroad tracks. Kiters turn left and then right until the end of the port buildings. Windsurfers, turn right and you'll reach Bob's Beach.

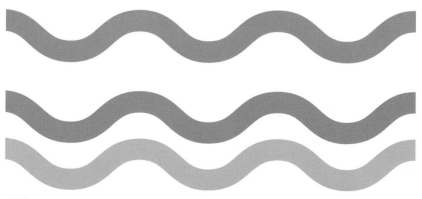

Kiting and Kids

Kiting and kids can be trouble, but if you use common sense and follow a few rules, you can have a wonderful family outing. Kite launch sites are windy, loud and hectic. Having children running around kites that are grounded or where kites are being launched and landed is dangerous for everyone. Please stay upwind of the kites and while one parent kites, make sure another adult keeps the kids away from the launch site.

CHAPTER 12

Indoor Fun

INDEPENDENT OF SUN

Photo by Clint Bogard

Twirling toddler

L ooking for indoor activities where you can stay dry on rainy days and avoid a sunburn on sunny days? How about going to a museum, attending storytime at the library, enrolling your kids in classes, painting pots or even bowling?

- Go Bowling
- Watch a Movie
- Read a Book
- Explore a Museum

Go Bowling

Orchard Lanes
🎳 *Hood River, OR*

Orchard Lanes has 16 lanes, some which are made for the novice bowler because the gutters can be blocked. They offer a youth rate for kids 17 and under, and host birthday parties. Be prepared to have a strikingly good time! 1141 Tucker Rd • (541) 386-1326 • www.orchardlanes.net

Watch a Movie

Cascade Cinema: 1410 W. 6th, The Dalles • (541) 298-2600 www.moviesinthedalles.com

Columbia Cinema: 2727 W. 7th St., The Dalles • (541) 296-8081 www.moviesinthedalles.com

Hood River Cinema: 5 5th Street, Hood River • (541) 386-7503 www.hoodrivercinemas.com

Skylight Theatre: Equipped with couches, serves pizza and is adult-only after 8:00 pm. 107 Oak St., Hood River • (541) 386-4888 www.skylighttheatre.com

Read a Book

Hood River Public Library
📍 *Hood River, OR*
Hours: Closed Sundays

Our library is one of the biggest buildings in town, and it's one of our favorite places to frequent, especially on a rainy day. The building has a large children's section and a separate room ideal for storytime and other activities. The friendly librarians tell stories on Thursdays at 10:30 in the morning. They also host a number of fun kid activities during the usual school breaks. See website for current offerings. 502 State St. • (541) 386-2535 • www.hoodriverlibrary.org

Stevenson Community Library
📍 *Stevenson, WA*
Hours: Closed Sundays

Stevenson Library seems to always have some interesting event for children whether it's the annual parade of poetry or teen game night. Story time is Wednesday and Thursday mornings at 10:30. 120 NW Vancouver Ave (509) 427-5471 • www.facebook.com/stevensonlibrary • www.fvrl.org

The Dalles Library
📍 *The Dalles, OR*
Hours: Closed Sundays

The Dalles Library has plans to expand their children section and construction will be underway very soon. They are even getting a new website. In the meantime, story time for newborns to 3 years old is on Wednesdays from 10:30-11:00 and on Friday mornings for preschoolers. 722 Court St • (541) 296-2815

White Salmon Public Library

White Salmon, WA

Hours: Closed Sundays

The children's story time at this library is outstanding, and often includes a special art craft. They host a separate story time for kids under three. It's a great place to meet other parents and compare notes about parenting. Story time is Wednesday and Thursday mornings. 5 Town and Country Square (509) 493-1132 • www.facebook.com/WhiteSalmonLibrary • www.fvrl.org

Bradford Island Visitor Center and Bonneville Fish Hatchery
Cascade Locks, OR
Hours: Open daily 9:00 to 5:00 pm

The Bradford Island Visitor Center has movies and displays about the dam and the various fish found in the Columbia with a focus on the salmon. You can watch the fish swim by the windows as you look into the fish ladder and learn about hydroelectric power in their display area. At the fish hatchery, make sure to stop in to see the 450 pound Herman the Sturgeon and feed the rainbow trout in the display ponds. During the fall salmon runs you can watch spawning activities; ie, killing and cutting open fish and harvesting the eggs and sperm. For a less brutal viewing process, watch the salmon spawn in one of the local streams like nearby Eagle Creek.

Getting There: Take I-84 to exit 40 (approximately 4 miles west of Cascade Locks) To get to the Fish Hatchery, at the flagpole intersection, bear left. Follow the road around to the large parking lot on the left. For the Bradford Island Visitor Center, turn right at the flagpole intersection. Follow the signs for approximately one mile along park roads.

Photo by Jurgen Hess

Columbia Gorge
Discovery Center
 The Dalles, OR
Hours: Open daily,
9:00 to 5:00 pm

Ready for the Oregon Trail

This extraordinary museum focuses on the natural and cultural history of the Gorge. One favorite exhibit helps you understand the challenges facing the pioneers on the Oregon Trail—should they navigate the Columbia River or traverse the Barlow trail? Taking you back to the mid-1800s, you learn about the Columbia River when it was sparkling clear, and full of salmon. Kids love playing in the dugout canoe, doing an art project in the small kids section, or trying on clothes from the 1800's when Lewis and Clark marched through the Gorge. Call ahead to check the schedule for the live raptor interpretive program when volunteers talk about various resident raptors including the great horned owl, bald eagle, American kestrel, red-tail hawk among others. Admission. $9 for adults; $5 for kids 6-16; free for kids 0-5. 5000 Discovery Dr (541) 296-8600 • www.gorgediscovery.org

Columbia Gorge Interpretive Center
Stevenson, WA
Hours: Open daily, 9:00 to 5:00 pm

This museum has life size exhibits including an indoor waterfall that will keep your kids entertained and even educate them about the Gorge. You'll see a 37-foot replica of a fish wheel, an operating steam engine, and explore artifacts from the Cascade Chinook tribe. There's an exceptional movie featuring the cataclysmic creation of the Gorge with dramatic pictures. The train outside allows you to explore a real steam engine—very exciting for the train lover in your family. You can also visit the outdoor replica of a gold mine complete with tools and wheeled cart. Admission is $10 for adults; $6 for kids 6-12; free for kids under six. 990 SW Rock Creek Dr
(509) 427-8211 • www.columbiagorge.org

Fort Dalles Historical Museum
The Dalles, OR
Hours: 7 days a week, 11-4; Closed in winter

Built in 1850, Fort Dalles was the only fort between Wyoming and the Pacific Coast. Constructed to protect the pioneers travelling west, the fort served as a logistics depot for military supplies. Today, the U.S. Army Surgeon's Headquarters is the only remaining structure and has been converted into a small museum full of local pioneer artifacts. Outside, there's a barn with antique cars, buggies and surries. Kids can ring the big bells on the cars. Make sure to call before as the museum is open at various times. Combine this with a visit to Sorosis Park, just up the hill, and you'll have a great afternoon. Admission, $5 for adults; 1$ for ages 7-17; 6 and under free. 500 W. 15th Street
(541) 296-2547 • www.fortdallesmuseum.org

History Museum of Hood River County
Hood River
Hours: Check website for hours

The History Museum hosts a variety of kid-focused activities throughout the year. Depending on the season, children will have fun picking apples, leaves and snowflakes, typing on an old fashioned typewriter, doing crafts and dressing up in period clothes. Ask the museum docent for a copy of their scavenger hunt—it's a clever and fun way for kids to explore the exhibits. They offer seasonal activities like summer camp, open house, family days and movie nights. Admission: free for kids 10 and under, active military and members; $5 for everyone else. 300 E. Port Marina Drive

(541) 386-6772 • www.co.hood-river.or.us/museum

Creative play space

Photo by Lisa Kosglow

Hutson Museum
Parkdale, OR
Hours: Open April-October; call for hours

This museum boasts a unique rock collection which looks likes a delicious meal. Don't eat it or you'll head straight to the dentist! The museum's hours coincide with the Mt. Hood Railroad train. If you are in Parkdale when the train's there or if you're on the train, this is a good quick stop. Admission: $1 for adults; $.50 for older kids. 4967 Baseline Dr. • (541) 352-6808

Maryhill Museum

📍 *Maryhill, WA*

Hours: 10:00 to 5:00 pm daily March 15 - December 15

What in Sam Hill is a museum doing in the middle of nowhere? The castle-like mansion was built in 1914 by Sam Hill, a wealthy entrepreneur and attorney who was also instrumental in constructing the Columbia River Highway. Sam built the mansion to lure his wife, Mary, out west. Mary never came and her home became a museum. The museum has a superb collection of chess sets and one of the largest displays of France's Auguste Rodin sculptures outside of Paris. There's a small cafe inside or you can picnic outside in the garden full of sculptures and meandering peacocks. Admission: Children 6 and under, free, youth $3 and adults $9.

Photo by Jan Meyer

This place is cool!

Getting There:
Take I-84 east 40 miles to Exit 104. Cross the Sam Hill Bridge into Washington and head north on Hwy. 97 until you reach Hwy. 14. Continue west for 3 miles. 35 Maryhill Museum Dr.

(509) 773-3733
www.maryhillmuseum.org

WAAAM Museum
Hood River, OR
Hours: Daily 9:00 to 5:00 pm

The Western Antique Aeroplane and Automobile Museum (WAAAM) contains one of the nation's largest collections of flying antique aeroplanes. What's even more impressive is that all the planes in the hangar fly. Director of the museum, Jeremy Young, says that he wouldn't have it otherwise—"that would be like going to the zoo and seeing stuffed animals." They also have a fleet of old cars taking you back in time. Our favorite is the T Tour Car, the same model as the one in Chitty Chitty Bang Bang. The museum created a new children's area, with a miniature submarine, helicopter, two person airplane, motorcycle and tractor. Here, unlike the other areas, kids can touch and romp around on the exhibits. Admission is free on the second Saturday of the month when historic planes fly overhead and you can even take a ride in one of the antique cars. Want more? Check out their summer WAAAM Camps for kids ages 9-12. Admission: $14 for adults; $6 for children 5-18; and free for children 4 and under.

1600 Air Museum Road
(541) 308-1600
www.waaamuseum.org

Girls cruising

Photo by Lisa Kosglow

WWF farm

Fun Jumpers
The Dalles
Hours: Varied, check Facebook page

Located behind Staples in The Dalles, Fun Jumpers is a popular indoor option for families with kids in need of burning off energy. A rotating array of inflatables keeps things changing. Kids can slide down the double bouncy slide, do WWF style tackles in the farm zone, play bouncy basketball and make believe in the bouncy castle. A small game room has foosball and air hockey and the adjacent party room has space for birthday parties. At the time of printing, Facebook is the best place to get information. If you're worried about older kids jumping over your little ones, look for pre-school only hours, usually on Wednesdays. 416 Cherry Heights Rd • (541) 769-0294

New Parent Services Playgroups
Cascade Locks, Hood River, Pine Grove, and The Dalles

Looking for a group of parents with kids the same age as yours? New Parent Services sponsors several free playgroups, which meet at varying times and places around the Gorge. Parents and caretakers are welcome.
(541) 436-0319 • www.nextdoorinc.org

Wonderworks Children's Museum of the Gorge
The Dalles, OR

If your kids are stir crazy, head east to the Wonderworks Children's Museum for oodles of indoor fun. A massive community effort in recent years has enabled Wonderworks to buy their own building and hire a few staff. The space is light filled, colorful and ready for young children 0 to 6 years old.

The community playroom has stations where children can play in the large playhouse, tend stuffed animals in the animal hospital, work on craft projects, create music, put on a play or puppet show, tumble in the soft cubes and mats, dig for dinosaur bones...whew! For the parents with infants wanting a respite from the frenzy, settle into the designated quiet area. They offer a variety of camps and classes. Daily admission $5 for all visitors over the age of 6 months or consider a yearly membership of $60 per family. Open Mon-Fri 9:30-4:30; Sat 9:30-1:00 pm. Check their website or facebook page for the most up to date information. 206 Madison St.
(541) 980-5922 • www.wonderworkschildrensmuseum.org

Photo Courtesy of Hood River County 4H

Kid Classes
Join 4-H

4-H (stands for Head, Heart, Hands and Health) is much more than the kids group that shows their animals at the County Fair. Kids can join a 4-H club and learn leadership skills through various activities like raising small animals and livestock, cooking, sewing, robotics, photography, babysitter trainings and leadership classes. You don't have to own an animal to join. For more information, take a look at the 4-H website, www.4-h.org, or call Dani Annala at the Hood River Extension. (541) 386-3343

Columbia Gorge Dance Academy
🏠 *Hood River*

The Columbia Gorge Dance Academy offers ballet, jazz, tap and hip hop classes. Classes are usually held during the school year from September to June, but they also have a few summer classes. If you have a budding dancer make sure to check out the Nutcracker (December) and Spring Recital (May) performances which feature dancers from Columbia Gorge Dance Academy and are fundraisers for local non-profits. 2600 May St. • (541) 386-3267 • www.columbiagorgedanceacademy.com

Gorge Grippers Family Nights
📍 *Hood River, OR*

Want to try climbing before investing in gear? Community Education offers a family climbing night at the Hood River Middle School climbing wall in the winter. Parents and kids learn how to tie knots, belay safely and use climbing commands. For eager climbers, join the Gorge Grippers team where kids hone their skills and gather for a number of climbing expeditions. Ages 6 and up. 1602 May St. • (541) 386-2055 • www.hrcommunityed.org

Gorge MakerSpace
📍 *Various*

Engineers in the making

A true gem in the Gorge and one that complements the loads of outdoor pursuits that we have here. Jack Perrin's MakerSpace classes are an ideal outlet for science and

Photo courtesy of Gorge MakerSpace

technology minded little inventors. The focus is on tinkering and making cool stuff, but kids also learn science and technology concepts along the way. Regular Wednesday afternoon classes are taught at the White Salmon Community Youth Center and he also offers classes at Gorge area libraries throughout the year. Check the website for current offerings.
(509) 808-1781 • www.gorgemakerspace.com

Gymnastics
Hood River Sports Club
📍 *Hood River, OR*

Let your kids focus on balance, coordination and strength in a gymnastics class at the Hood River Sports Club. Tumblers, Twisters, Kinderoos and beyond. Classes are open to children ages 2 and up. Parents join toddlers, but then they soon summersault on their own. 1330 Brookside Dr.
(541) 386-3230 • www.hoodriversportsclub.com/gymnastics

Riverside Gymnastics Academy
The Dalles, OR

Kids can balance, roll and tumble away all under the eyes of exceptional instructors. Preschool classes, recreational classes and more serious elite teams are all available. Children 4 and under can drop in on Tuesdays and Fridays for Kindergym with parent supervision. Summer classes and birthday parties also available. 2221 River Road • (541)993-8625 • www.riverside-gym.org

Kids Yoga

Flow Yoga Studio
Hood River, OR

Yoga is an excellent way for kids to learn about their bodies and their calmer selves. While your children are doing their downward facing dogs, you can practice the Eagle Pose in a separate class. Need help on Spring Break or Summer Break? Flow offers kids yoga camps. Have a bun in the oven? Check out the pregnancy classes. 118 Third St. (541) FUNYOGA • www.flowhoodriver.com

Namaste

Photo by Scott Rumsey

Learn a Martial Art

Aikido

📍 *Hood River, OR*

Inside Trinity Natural Medicine, young martial artists learn the "way of harmonious spirit" with Sensei Neil Lofgren who teaches children to protect themselves while taking care not to hurt their attacker. Unlike other martial arts, aikido is not combative. Instead of punching and kicking, kids learn how to move their body in relationship to someone else, how to keep their balance and how to fall down without getting hurt. There's the added bonus of learning to count in Japanese and the names for key concepts. Most important, they learn to coordinate and control their body through fun movement games and tumbling. 1801 Belmont St. • (541) 386-2025 • www.facebook.com/gorgebudo

Tae Kwan Do

📍 *Hood River, OR*

There are two studios in Hood River for kids to study the Korean martial art of Tae Kwan Do, loosely translated to "foot and hand way." Students learn the controlled kicks and some can even break wood with their bare hands. Classes are held during the year. Both schools are in the Heights and Northwest Tae Kwon Do has a location in The Dalles.

Hood River Martial Arts: 1016 11th St. (541) 490-4344
www.hoodrivermartialarts.com

Northwest Tae Kwon Do:
1203 12th St.
(541) 387-3222

1925 W 2nd Street, The Dalles
(541) 387-3222

Bryce testing for his next belt.

Photo by Kevin Donald www.columbiagorgeimages.com

Music Classes

Mary Ann Hall's Music For Children
Hood River, OR

Photo courtesy of Molly Schwartz

Kids love teacher Molly Schwarz because she's fun and magnetic. Classes for the little ones (infants to age 3) are for both parents and their children. Older kids (up to 7 years) can be dropped off at Molly's whimsical music studio. 1115 Hull St., Hood River (541) 490-1518 www.musicforchildrenor.com

Gorge Musik
White Salmon, WA

Experienced Kindermusik teacher Jennifer Harty has created her own style of teaching at Gorge Musik. Children 18 months to 4 years old play, sing and dance in classes. 240 NW Washington • (541) 716-1331 • www.gorgemusik.com

Hood River Community Education

The Community Education Bulletin is a goldmine, filled with amazing opportunities for kids. Pick up a copy at the Hood River Public Library, Community Education Office or check their online class list. You'll find tons of great classes for kids from outdoor adventure camps, to soccer, art, cooking and more. (541) 386-2055, www.hrcommunityed.org

Survival hut

CHAPTER 13

SIGN UP FOR

Summer Camps

Analyzing the water

Summer is great opportunity for kids to explore their interests and find their passions. Below are some of the camps that we think might interest your kids. This is not an exhaustive list and we urge you to visit the Hood River Community Ed website, www.hrcommunityed.org.

Adventure and Outdoor Exploration Camps

Cascade Mountain School
📍 *Trout Lake, WA*

Cascade Mountain School offers science based camps for middle and high schoolers. Our backyard is a rich classroom for students to learn about food systems, fisheries, energy productions and more. High schoolers can jump start next year's school requirements and earn credit the fun way, from the science camps. www.cascademountainschool.org

Hood River Community Education
📍 *Hood River, OR*

Hood River Community Education is a gold mine of kids activities in the summer. Community Ed's flagship program, the two week Summer Day Camp, is one of the only camps that takes place all day and accommodates parents work schedule. Moreover it is affordable. Look to the paper catalog or search classes online. www.hrcommunityed.org

Wanna climb?

Let's Get Out Adventure and Exploration Camps
📍 Hood River, OR

Want your child to be outside during the summer? Let's Get Out offers a variety of adventure and explorer camps for children ages 5 to 13 years old. The older kids, the Explorers, play outside and rock climb, mountain bike, hike, spelunk and white water raft all while honing their wilderness awareness skills. Campers learn teamwork, Leave No Trace ethics and participate in a stewardship project. Groups are small just 6-10 kids. The younger, 5-7 year old Explorers, get a combination of guided exploration utilizing nature based activities like exploring aquatic insects and mammals that live in the Gorge, play awareness games and work on an art project. (541) 400-9061 • www.lets-get-out.com

Mt Hood Meadows Outdoor Education and Adventure Summer Camp
📍 Mt. Hood Meadows, OR

This education program for 7-14 year olds focuses on fostering a connection between young people and the natural world. The camp teaches campers about the varied environment on Mt Hood, including volcanoes, glaciers, waterways, plants and animals. In addition to the educational components, kids will also hike, raft and swim. www.skihood.com

Smith Rocks Climbing Camp
📍 *Smith Rock State Park, OR*

We are fortunate to have two incredibly experienced climbing guides, Lisa and John Rust, in our community who have climbed some of the most rugged mountains in the world, including Mt. Everest. They bring kids 9 years and older for a week of climbing at Smith Rocks, a renowned climbing crag near Bend. Kids learn to set up top ropes, lead climb and scale the classics, like Dihedrals, Morning Glory and Monkey Face.
(541) 490-9104 • www.hrcommunityed.com

Scaling Monkey Face

Photo courtesy of Hood River Community Education

Photo by Robin Dickenson

Lights, camera, action

Art and Theater Camps

The CAST Theater and Gallery has a number of art experiences for kids of all ages ranging from theater, to painting to weaving.
• (541) 387-8877
www.columbiaarts.org

Thespians from 8 to 18 years old work with Rebekah Meyers and perform a summer musical at Jackson Park. • www.hrcommunityed.org.

Young actors, ages 4 to 12, can also get on stage with Heather Laurance at the Mt. Hood Town Hall. • (541) 645-0351 • www.mt.hoodtownhall.org

Gorge Creations is another fun place for young artists from 4 to 12 years old who come for the day or multiple days during the summer.
(541) 386-2373 • www.gorgecreations.com

The Gorge Art Farm has art classes for children ages 4 to 8.
(541) 716-5273 • www.gorgeartfarm.org

Bike Camps

Cooper Spur Mt. Bike Club
Area: Hood River, OR

For kids wanting to take their riding to the next level, try the Cooper Spur Mt Bike Club. Kids work on drills and technique while exploring trails at Post Canyon. Riders must be 10 to 15 years old and have strong bike skills to participate. www.cooperspurraceteam.org/mountain-bike

Peace Camp
Columbia Gorge Peace Village
🅐1 *Hood River, OR*

Who doesn't want peace? Kids ages 6-13 play, create, sing and dance all while learning about non-violent traditions around the world. Kids return year after year to this well loved Gorge summer camp.
www.columbiagorgepeacevillage.com

Give peace a chance

Kayaking the Klickitat

Rafting/Kayaking Camps

📍 Hood River, OR and BZ Corners, WA

Our rivers are wild and scenic—is that a cliche? But it's true and one of the best ways to enjoy the White Salmon or Klickitat is to kayak or raft down it. The Cascadia Kayak School offers a variety of day camps as well as an overnight camp for kayakers at least 9 years old. www.cascadia.org. Wet Planet in BZ Corners also has a youth program and a variety of skill clinics. (877) 390-9445 • www.wetplanetwhitewater.com

Sailing Camps

📍 Hood River and Cascade Locks, OR

GORGE Junior Sailing has a variety of camps and classes for novice to advanced sailors. Sign up through Hood River Community Ed, www.hrcommunityed.org. If you want to test the waters and see if your child is interested in sailing, come down on Monday nights in August and jump in a boat. Cascade Locks, one of the premier places to race dinghies in the country, also offers sailing classes. See cgra.org. (see also our sailing section in the Extreme Sports Chapter)

Photo courtesy of Gorge Sailing School

Ski and Snowboard Camps

🎿 Mt. Hood, OR

The year round snow on Timberline makes it possible to have a number of ski and snowboard summer camps, including:

High Cascade Snowboard Camp: (503) 206-8520
www.highcascade.com

Mt. Hood Summer Ski Camp: (503) 337-2230 • www.mthood.com

Timberline Ski Resort: Race and freestyle ski and snowboard camps
(503) 222-2211 • www.timberlinelodge.com

Windells: Snowboard, freeski and skateboard camps.
(800) 765-7669 • www.windells.com

Bend Endurance Academy: Nordic racers can sign up with the Bend Endurance Academy for an intensive roller ski and epic off trail adventure camp in Trout Lake.
(541) 480-4563 • www.bendenduranceacademy.org

>>> Dropping!

Windsurfing and Kite Camps

Big Winds: Big Winds has a popular windsurfing camp for kids 7 to 13 years old. Their camp takes place at the Hook, one of the few places in the Gorge protected from the wind. (888) 509-4210 • www.bigwinds.com

Cascade Kiteboarding: For kiteboarding, Cascade Kiteboarding has a few summer camps for kids 9 to 18 years old. It's impressive how the young kids with no fear can learn to kite so quickly. Parents can rest easy knowing that the camps are jet ski assisted. (541) 392-1212 • www.cascadekiteboarding.com

Shaka!

Fiona Wylde, Champion of Extreme Water Sports

The Gorge is home to numerous successful young athletes such as in-spirational Fiona Wylde. Once Fiona learned to swim, her father placed her on the nose of his windsurfer and when she was 6 years old, she had figured out how to windsurf on her own. Fiona started racing at 11 and kiting at 12. A competitive "water girl," she has won many windsurfing and stand up paddling events. Thanks to online high school (which she completed in May 2015), she competes and trains around the world in windsurfing, kiting, and SUPing. She's our local rockstar!

CHAPTER 14

WE ALL SCREAM FOR
Ice Cream

Photo by Lisa Kosglow

I scream, you scream...

Your kids will probably place this category on the top of your "to do" list. Sometimes our children even scream for ice cream before breakfast. Yes, for some of us, ice cream is a necessity in life. If not an outing on its own, ice cream stops go hand-in-hand with a waterfall hike or an escape from one of our hot summer days. Here's the scoop.

Alabama Jim's Long Shot

Parkdale, OR

Year round

Named for the former owner's dead father-in-law, who worked as a chef for general's in the military, Alabama Jim's is a classic ice cream store. They serve Umpqua, Tillamook and Cascade Glacier Farm ice cream. Try their licorice ice cream, and your tongue may never be the same. Just take a look at the dramatic pictures inside! This hang-out also serves sandwiches, soups and other lunch food. If you are in Parkdale looking for a treat, look no further!

Getting There: Drive 13 miles south on Hwy. 35, turn right onto Cooper Spur Rd. Drive another two miles and turn right on Baseline Dr., into town.
4946 Baseline Dr.
(541) 352-3553

Photo by Lisa Kosglow

Sweet with a cherry on top

Photo by Lisa Kosglow

Big Jim's Drive In

The Dalles, OR

Year round

"Hamburgers Made with Love," that's the Big Jim's slogan and they're also making banana splits, sundaes, smoothies and shakes with love too! In fact, they've been serving burgers and cold treats to ice cream lovers for 47 years. With sixteen flavors of Umpqua hard ice cream plus soft serve, everyone will be satisfied.

Getting There: Drive east on I-84 towards The Dalles and take Exit 87. Turn right off the exit ramp and take the next right onto US 30. Turn right onto E. 2nd St. and you'll see Big Jim's on your right. 2938 E. 2nd St • (541) 298-5051

Apple Valley Country Store

Hood River, OR

Season: Closed in winter, varied hours other seasons

This country classic situated right at the Hood River's bend has the best fruit shakes around made with real fruit! Choose from huckleberry, marionberry, strawberry and more! Not in the mood for a shake, sample their jams, jellies and mustards or eat apple pie. They have an outdoor BBQ in the summer.

Getting There: From Cascade Ave., turn right on 13th St. and drive 5 miles south on 12th St., which becomes Tucker Rd. 2363 Tucker Rd. (541) 386-1971 • www.applevalleystore.com

Granny Gedunk's Ice Cream Parlor

Stevenson, WA

Closed in winter, varied hours other seasons

This classic ice cream parlor serves Umpqua Ice Cream and donuts. If Granny or the likes of her scoops the servings, then you're in luck—they're substantial. Try the homemade waffle cones or the milkshakes. Every town needs an ice cream parlor like this one.

Getting There: From Hood River, drive east on I-84 to Exit 44. Cross the Bridge of the Gods and turn right on Hwy. 14. Continue until you drive reach town. 196 SW Second St. • (509) 427-4091

Cicci Gelato

Hood River, OR

Closes when the rain comes, opens with the sun in late spring

Photo by Blaine Franger • www.blaineandbethany.com

Loving Cicci!

Cicci is a new ice cream food cart, that often parks at the waterfront right next to Solstice. The owner, Theresa makes artisanal, hand-crafted gelato and sorbettos fresh daily with organic milk and fresh fruit. Her servings are smaller, which works especially for little kids.

Getting There: Take N. 2nd north to the river, make a left on Portway and you'll see the cart next to Solstice Pizza. 603 Portway Ave. • (541) 490-2411

Eastwind Drive In

📍 *Cascade Locks, OR*
☀ *Open year round*

If you're looking to cool off with melt-in-the-mouth soft serve ice cream, then this is the place for you. Some rave that it's better than Dairy Queen. They also serve fast food burgers and fries. Dessert first?

🧭 **Getting There:** From Hood River, drive 16 miles west on I-84 to Exit 44, Cascade Locks. Continue one mile into town and the Drive In is on the right side. 395 Wa-Na-Pa St. • (541) 374-8380

😋 Mike's Ice Cream

📍 *Hood River, OR*
🌙☀❄ *Closed in Winter*

On a hot day, our kids vote Mike's the best place to eat ice cream in the Gorge. They serve Prince Pucklers' ice cream made in Eugene. The area of this adorable ice cream shack and the atmosphere makes you want to come back again and again. While you're licking your scoop, check out the bulletin board to find out what's happening in town. Make sure to bring cash—credit cards and checks aren't accepted.

🧭 **Getting There:** On the main drag just across the street from the library. 504 Oak St. (541) 386-6260

Photo by Clint Bogard

Route 30 Classics and Roadside Refreshments
🅟 *Mosier, OR*
🌙 ☀ ❄ *Closed in winter*

This super cool ice cream store is one-of-a-kind. What other ice cream store cohabitates with a Porsche dealership? Enjoy your Umpqua ice cream sitting on the high bar stools along the window overlooking the main road of the sleepy town of Mosier. If you have enough money in the piggy bank, you could leave not only with a satisfied sweet tooth, but also a stylin' Porsche. We like to combine ice cream with a bike ride on the Mosier Tunnels trail for a stellar outing.

🧭 **Getting There:** Drive east on I-84 to Exit 69. Make a right at the end of the off-ramp and follow Route 30 until you see the store. 1100 1st Ave., Mosier • (541) 478-2525 • www.route30classics.com

Mother's Marketplace
🅟 *Hood River, OR*
☀ *Open all year*

We've added this to our chapter even though it isn't ice cream but for the non dairy child, head to Mothers and Margaret will make you Lisa's favorite, a berry smoothie. Adults can enjoy the locally brewed kombucha and water kefir on tap.

🧭 **Getting There:** From downtown Hood River, head east to Hwy. 35 and make a left just passed the four way stop sign. Continue towards the river and turn left into the Windance Parking Lot. 106 Hwy. 35 • (541) 387-2202 • www.mothersmarketplace.net

Troutdale General Store
🔴 *Troutdale, OR*

The Troutdale General Store feels like a step back into the 1950's with its old-fashioned wooden dining counter and classic stools. It's awesome to sit here and share a classic ice cream sundae. Oma believes its the best Sundae she's had in her life. In addition to ice cream (they sell Cascade Glacier Ice Cream), you can also get breakfast or lunch. The store bursts with gift items, candy, home decorations and much more.

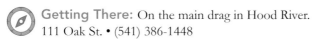 **Getting There:** Because of its proximity to Portland, directions will be from the west. Take I-84 east to Marine Drive, Exit 17, NW Frontage Road until Graham Rd., turn right at the Old Columbia Hwy. and the General Store will be on the left side. 289 E Historic Columbia River, Troutdale (503) 492-7912

Yum Fro Yo
🔴 *Hood River, OR*

A popular self serve frozen yogurt with various flavors, like raspberry pomegranate sorbet and peach tart. It's fun to sample flavors and add yummy toppings. Kai, of course, likes to add heaps of sweets, like the reese's peanut butter pieces and gummy bears. Don't forget the hot fudge! Hard to hold back on the yummy treats.

Getting There: On the main drag in Hood River. 111 Oak St. • (541) 386-1448

Kids Being Creative

Thanks to Gorge Soup (a local group encouraging entrepreneurs), Kai Rayle, 11 at the time, received $500 to construct a solar powered ice cream cart. Together with his sister and friends, he created Kai's Cones using four recycled windsurfing masts, a fruit cart, and a solar panel which they connected to a battery that powers the freezer and keeps the ice cream cold. During the summer, the kids pedal around the Gorge selling their tasty homemade ice cream sandwiches. Look for them on the waterfront.

CHAPTER 15

Happenings

AROUND THE HOOD

Magical night at Jackson Park

Rich with community events, the Gorge has tons of fun and interesting happenings, whether it's music in the park, a festival, or the County Fair. What follows is not an exhaustive list, but rather hones in on the festivities that the whole family will enjoy.

First Fridays

 Hood River, OR

First Friday of the month from March-December

On the first Friday beginning at 5:00 pm of every month from March until December, local artists team up with downtown stores to exhibit their masterpieces. Many stores serve food and wine and stay open until 8:00 pm. Musicians play and onlookers dance. Sometimes the street is closed to car traffic. Bring your family, stroll the street and bump into your friends. One of the First Fridays features an outdoor chalk drawing contest, which our kids love. There's always something fun for kids.

Getting There: First Fridays is celebrated on Oak and Cascade Streets in downtown Hood River

Mt. Hood Meadows Kids Carnival

 Mt. Hood, OR

Mid-March

Our local ski resort hosts an annual snow carnival usually during spring break. There's a huge ice castle with a slide to climb on and sled down, an obstacle course, races, and live music.

Getting There: Travel south on Hwy. 35 for 32 miles, until the Mt. Hood Meadows Resort.
(800) SKI-HOOD • www.skihood.com

April

Earth Day
📷 *Hood River, OR*
Mid-April

Earth Day is a big deal in the Gorge because we love our earth and want to combat global warming. Many local organizations host kid friendly events, like weeding the waterfront park and picking up trash. Check out www.gorge-owned.org for Earth Day volunteer opportunities.

Photo by Paloma Ayala • www.fotoisphoto.com

Bolting through the blossoms

Hood River Valley Blossom Festival
📷 *Hood River Valley, OR*
Third weekend in April

When the blossoms bloom, thousands of people flock to the Hood River Valley to celebrate their arrival. Featuring art and music, antique, quilt and craft shows, and farm tours, the festival takes place all over the valley. Kids love running around in the orchards—especially when the apple, pear and cherry trees look they are covered with white and pink popcorn. Hood River Fruit Loop (800) 366-3530 • www.hoodriver.org • www.hoodriverfruitloop

The Dalles Cherry Festival
📷 *The Dalles, OR*
Third weekend in April

The Dalles cheers on the cherry blossoms with heaps of festivities, including a parade, food contest, dance party, bike ride and much more. It's a festive welcome and very fun for kids. (800) 255-3385 • www.thedalleschamber.com

May
😊 Hood River Farmers Market
📍 *Hood River, OR*
Thursdays every week from May to November

Photo by Blaine Franger • www.blaineandbethany.com

Molly the pied piper

A weekly tradition, the Hood River Farmers Market is a tasty place to be on Thursday evenings. Families can find nourishing, tasty dinner options, pick out their weekly produce, breads, cheese and meats, dance to free music, and play on the grassy hillside. During the summer, the market sets up at the Hood River Middle School and then moves to Springhouse Cellars, near the Mt. Hood Railroad. Please check www.gorgegrown.com for updates and a list of the other Gorge Farmers Markets.

Hood River Saturday Market
📍 *Hood River, OR*
Saturday 10:00 to 2:00 pm from June-September

Every Saturday morning, farmers bring their produce and artists sell their wares at the market. Held in a small parking lot on the main drag, the market is a place to see what the local artists are up to as well as buy some fresh eggs, fruit and cheese. It's more of a craft market than a farmer's market but that could change.

 Getting There: On 4th ant Oak St. at the parking lot of the Horse & Hound British Pub Lot (4th & Oak St.).
(541) 490-6420 • www.gorgegrown.com

Columbia Gorge Dance Academy's Spring Recital

Hood River, OR

Mid-May

The Columbia Gorge Dance Academy puts on an impressive spring recital where students perform ballet, tap, hip hop and jazz. For a small town, we have incredible talent and very supportive families. The performance usually happens at the Hood River Middle School on May St.
(541) 386-3267 • www.columbiagorgedanceacademy.com

White Salmon Spring Fest

White Salmon, WA

End of May

This three-day festival gives a small town welcome to the spring flowers and warm weather. Kids dress up for the parade, get their faces painted, laugh with the clowns and dance to music.
(509) 365-4565 • www.whitesalmonspringfestival.com

June

Passport to Fishing Day at Bonneville Fish Hatchery

Bonneville Dam, OR

Early June

Ready to catch the big one? The Bonneville Fish Hatchery opens its waters to kids 12 and under. You don't have to bring a thing...for fishing, that is. Kids are given loaner fishing poles, and there's plenty of fish to catch and other fish-oriented activities.

Mt. Adams Country Bike Tour—Family Ride

Trout Lake, WA
Saturday at the end of June

Bring the family and pedal the 11.5 miles on the country roads in Trout Lake Valley. They have longer 50 and 100 plus miles, but this shorter one is perfect for young families. The ride is fully supported with sag wagons and food. www.troutlakewashington.com

July

Fourth of July in Hood River

Hood River, OR
4th of July

Put on your red, white and blue, get an old car, unicycle or fire truck, and enter the parade! This small town celebration weaves down 13th Street and ends with music, hot dogs and apple pie at Jackson Park. If you don't want to be in the parade, you can watch from the sidelines and cheer the floats on. In the evening, head down to the Marina to watch the fireworks.

Fort Dalles Pro Rodeo

The Dalles, OR
Mid-July

Cowgirls, cowboys, wild broncos and bulls—the rodeo is full of dust, music, food, dancing, tournaments, parades and even a queen who oversees the crowd. Come see the pros rope the calves and ride the bulls— just don't try it yourself! Thursday is Family Night, offering a discount for the whole family.

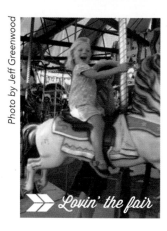

Lovin' the fair

Hood River County Fair

Location: Odell, OR
When: Mid-July

Rides, animals, music and some of the best fair food around! Lisa's favorite food booth is Mama Nina's Cocina where Gavina Rivera and her sisters make fresh tortillas and their signature dish, Corundas. Don't miss this slice of Americana.
3020 Wy'east Rd., Hood River
(541) 354-2865 • www.hoodriverfair.com

Columbia Gorge Bluegrass Festival

Stevenson, WA
Late July

Can't make it to String Summit? This is the Gorge's version, held at the fairgrounds in Stevenson. Music all day and nightly dances make sure everyone get's their boogie on. It's fun to camp at the Event Site or visit for just one day. www.columbiagorgebluegrass.net

August

Movies in the Park

Hood River, OR
Saturdays at dusk; end of July and August

Hood River Community Ed runs lots of great programs, including Movies in the Park. We love to bring our blankets and stretch out under the trees at Jackson Park and watch a kid friendly movie on the big screen.

 Families in the Park Concert Series
📍 *Hood River, OR*
7:00 pm every Thursday in August

Every Thursday night in August, it seems like all of Hood River gathers for a concert at Jackson Park. Food vendors start selling at 6:00 pm and music starts at 7:00 pm. Come early to stake out a plot of grass as the park fills up fast. Bring lawn chairs, bug spray, a picnic and be ready to dance.

Skamania County Fair and Timber Carnival
📍 *Stevenson*
Mid-August

This fair prides itself on being a less commercial fair and a more community fair. The 4-H kids show their animals and the farmers share their secret preserves and berry pies. This is one of the only fairs where admission is free. www.skamaniacounty.org

Columbia Gorge Paddle Challenge
📍 *Hood River, OR*
Third week in August

SUPers take over the Columbia River in August for one of the most competitive SUP races in the country. For kids 17 and under, Pro SUPer Kai Lenny teaches a clinic before a number of SUP events. The kids portion is a huge success, with more than 200 young SUPers jumping on boards.

September

Timberline Labor Day Mountain Music Festival
📍 **Mt Hood, OR**
Labor Day

Free music, huckleberry shakes and incredible views. What's not to love? It's a special way to spend a sunny September day. Head up early to dance with your kids and if you have an instrument—people are jammin' on the patio. Music plays all day long. (503) 272-3134 • www.timberline.lodge.com

Hood River Fly-In
📍 **Hood River**
First weekend following Labor Day

For kids and adults that love planes, this event is not to be missed. The Fly-In celebrates the bird's eye view of our surroundings. The airport and the WAAM Museum hosts all sorts of planes, from model airplanes to gliders to biplanes. The location of the Fly-In alternates yearly between Hood River and The Dalles.

Gorge Kids Triathlon
📍 **Hood River**
   Waterfront Park
Usually the third Sunday in September

Photo by Ray Perkins

The Gorge Kids Triathlon was created in 2011 by a group of local parents who wanted to provide a healthy activity for kids and also raise funds for PE programs in the schools. It's been a huge success with more than 300 kids from Kindergarten to 5th Grade participating. See their website for more information. www.gorgekidstri.com

Huckleberry Festival

📍 Bingen, WA
Early September

The City of Bingen kicks off this festival with a small town parade featuring fire trucks, old cars, politicians and floats. Everyone ends up at the park for food, music and carnival rides and huckleberry pie.

Festival of Nations

📍 Cascade Locks, OR
End of September

Together with the Warm Springs Tribe, the city of Cascade Locks opens up the Marina Park to ethnic dancers, food, music and games for the kids. There's even a run for the athletic souls and some great dancing and drumming. www.festivalofnations.info

October

Hood River Valley Harvest Festival

📍 Hood River Valley, OR
Third weekend in October

This popular festival celebrates apples, pears, pumpkins, and the fall. Down at the Expo Center, you'll find artisans, musicians and delicious food. At the Fairgrounds in Odell, you can buy fruit and vegetables from the local farmers. In Parkdale, you'll find a market with artists, bands, and food. Grab a Fruit Loop map and travel from farm-to-farm and make sure to stop at Kiyokawa Orchard's for family fun.

Trick or treat?

Halloween: The Gorge loves Halloween so much that you might think about having a variety of Halloween costumes. For pumpkin picking, journey to The Dalles' Renken Farm. Put on a costume and join the Parkdale Pumpkin Parade. Trick or Treating in downtown Hood River is a safe exciting place to be. Please see our Pumpkin Section in Chapter 7, Hanging out in the Orchards.

December

The Nutcracker: Thanks to Nancy Clement, Susan Sorenson and all the teachers at the Dance Academy, the Nutcracker performance is a must-see with incredible costumes and huge smiles on the dancers as they pirouette on stage, making every parent proud. Performances are at the Hood River Middle School.

Hood River Tree Lighting:

This is a super fun family event centered around lighting the tall tree on State and 2nd Streets. There's a parade, hot chocolate and carollers singing "Deck the Halls." This community event sets the mood for the Holiday Season.

Columbia Gorge Hotel Lights: In true holiday spirit, the grand Columbia Gorge Hotel lights their gardens with thousands of white lights. We love to stroll their grounds and marvel at their 200 foot waterfall, that plunges down, down, down into the river.

4000 Westcliff Dr. • (800) 345-1921 • www.columbiagorgehotel.com

Other Holiday Happenings

• Hood River Hotel: Don't miss their festive tree decorating evening featuring music, carolers and the man with the beard.

• Skamania Lodge: Decorate a gingerbread house and learn from the chefs who make an intricate gingerbread village.

CHAPTER 16

Childcare, Babysitting & Breastfeeding

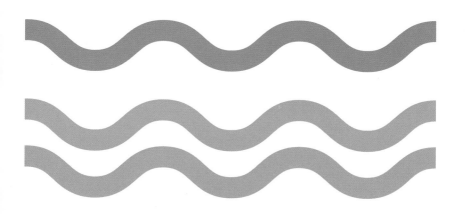

One of our biggest challenges as parents is finding good, reliable help. When choosing a babysitter or daycare center, make sure to thoroughly check out the person or place before leaving your child.

GorgeKids.com Website: This valuable website not only offers information about events and activities for families in the Gorge, but it also has a section for finding babysitters and daycare providers. www.gorgekids.com

Gorge.Net Website: The classified section is an excellent way to search for babysitters or even post your needs. You can also look for other things you may need, like a bike, a kite, or a place to call home.

Our Children's Place: Owner Teacher Janet has a wealth of experience to share with you and your kids. She's also a local tv star on KATU - 2, providing tips on parenting and children's activities. A preschool and daycare, Our Children's Place offers special kid classes, drop in care and after school care during the school year, when Teacher Janet and her staff help with homework. Call for various options. 1110 12th St., Suite B
(541) 386-1975 • www.teacherjanet.com

Rachel's Corner: Offers childcare for infants 6 weeks to 4 year olds. Drop-ins are welcome when space is available. Rachel and her mother have teamed together for more than 10 years. (541) 386-5993 • www.rachelscorner.com.

Support Groups: The Gorge Breastfeeding Support Group meets every other Wednesday at the Riverside Community Church in Hood River. 317 State St. • (541) 387-6344.

CHAPTER 17

KID-FRIENDLY

Restaurants

Photo by Blaine Franger • www.blaineandbethany.com

Dinner!

Would you like to enjoy a meal out where you can get a highchair, paper and crayons, maybe some toys or enough background noise that no one is bothered by your children? Here are some of the restaurants in and around the Gorge where you won't have to cringe when you walk in with the whole brood. Bon Appetit!

What is a kid-friendly restaurant? A restaurant that has made a concerted effort to cater to families because they recognize the challenge of eating out with small children. For the most part, almost all of the restaurants in the Gorge are kid-friendly. We categorized the list into coffeehouses, breakfast places, dinner spots, outdoor seating, playground restaurants, quick bites and food to go. We thought this highlighted each restaurant's best quality in terms of kid-friendliness. Please recognize that not everything fits tidy into a category. If you want to bring the family to some of the finer establishments, we suggest going early and not on a weekend

Breakfast Places

Best Western Hood River Inn: Consider Sunday brunch on their deck overlooking the river. 1108 East Marina Way, Hood River (541) 386-2200 • www.hoodriverinn.com

Bette's Place: A classic breakfast place with hometown cooking and famous cinnamon buns. They love kids and don't cry over spilled milk. 416 Oak St. (541) 386-1880 • www.bettesplace.com

Egg Harbor Cafe: Serves a hearty breakfast in booths where kids can hide away. 1313 Oak Street, Hood River • (541) 386-1127

Good News Gardening: Eating in their cafe feels like being in an elegant living room with tasty organic food. 1086 Tucker Rd., Hood River (541) 386-6438 • www.goodnewsgardening.com

River Daze: Breakfast of blueberry pancakes, homemade English muffins to write home about and bacon waffles. Big tables and plenty of space. 202 Oak Street, Hood River • (541) 386-9404 • www.riverdazecafe.com

Windseeker: This restaurant has a 1950s feel. The Belgian waffles combined with the river view and garden with carp in the ponds makes for a great breakfast. 1535 Bargeway Rd., The Dalles
(541) 298-7171 • www.windseekerrestaurant.com

Coffeehouses

10-Speed Coffee Bar: The Coffee Bar has cool bicycle chairs and a space upstairs where kids can play freely. 1412 13th St., Hood River
(541) 386-3165 • www.10speedcoffee.com

Bahma Coffee Bar: Bahma in Hebrew means "one's place of personal comfort." This local hot spot lives up to its name. 77 Russell Ave., Stevenson
(509) 427-8700 • www.bahmacoffeebar.com

Dog River: This popular coffee hang-out has comfortable couches in the back and games and toys for kids. 411 Oak St., Hood River
(541) 386-4502 • www.dogrivercoffee.com

Ground: Stop in for a baked treat or the great tea selection.
12 Oak Street, Hood River • (541) 386-4442

Doppio: Tasty sandwiches, coffee and kids can cool off at the fountain.
310 Oak St., Hood River • (541) 386-3000 • www.doppiohoodriver.com

Stoked Roasters and Coffeehouse: Grab a cup of jo while your kids play at the waterfront park. 603 Portway Ave., Hood River
(303) 870-8186 • www.stokedroasters.com

The Good Medicine Lounge: Tea lovers rejoice! The options are mind boggling and there's a little play table for kids in one corner.
1029 May St., Hood River • (541) 436-2540

Dinner/Lunch Spots

Apple Valley BBQ: Tim says its the best bbq in the Gorge. The meat is smoked with local cherry wood. 4956 Baseline Dr., Parkdale (541) 352-3554 • www.applevalleybbq.com

Big River Grill: Modern day roadhouse with classic burgers, historic photos and other interesting things to gaze at inside. 192 SW 2nd St., Stevenson (509) 427-4888 • www.bigrivergrill.com

Casa El Mirador: Delicious Mexican food and quick service. 302 W. 2nd St., The Dalles (541) 298-7388 • www.casaelmirador.com

China Gorge: Kai loves the General Tso's chicken. The chow mein and potstickers are also a hit. 2680 Old Columbia River Hwy., Hood River (541) 386-5331 • www.chinagorge.com

CharBurger: Amazing views of The Bridge of the Gods and the river, tasty burgers and marionberry pie. 745 NW Wanapa St., Cascade Locks (541) 374-8477

Cousins Restaurant: This diner-style restaurant has a miniature train and farm animals that don't have to be fed. 2114 W. 6th Street, The Dalles (541) 298-2771 • www.cousinsthedalles.com

Crazy Pepper Cantina: It seems like the minute you enter this Mexican restaurant with kids in hand, crayons and chips and salsa will be at your table. 103 4th Street, Hood River • (541) 387-2454 • www.thecrazypeppercantina.com

Double Mountain Hood River: Popular beer and pizza, go early to avoid crowds. 8 Fourth St., Hood River (541) 387-0042 • www.doublemountainbrewery.com

El Puerto de Angeles: A Mexican restaurant in the Heights with big portions, comfortable booths, and quick service. Kids get books as soon as they sit down. 1306 12th St., Hood River • (541) 308-0005

El Rio Mexican Cafe: Good Mexican/American food, especially the fajitas and chile rellenos. 193 SW 2nd St., Stevenson • (509) 427-4479

Hennis Kitchen and Bar: 120 E. Jewett Blvd., White Salmon (509) 493-1555 • www.henniskitchenandbar.com

Hood River Hotel's Vintage Grill: Our local hotel on the main street serves southern soul food. Come early with the kids. 102 Oak Avenue, Hood River • (541) 386-1900 • www.thevintagegrille.com

Killer Burger: French fries included with every burger. 216 W. Steuben, Bingen, WA • (509) 637-2510 • www.killerburger.biz

Mesquitery: Come hungry for barbequed ribs, chicken or steaks. 1219 12th St., Hood River • (541) 386-2002

Michoacan Sports Bar & Grill: Delicious authentic carnitas. 3405 Odell Hwy., Odell • (541) 354-2900 • www.michogrill.com

Petite Provence: Savor a taste of France, delicious patisseries, croissants and bistro food. 408 E. 2nd St., The Dalles (541) 506-0037 • www.provencepdx.com

Pfreim Family Brewers: Good burgers, big tables for families and tasty beer for mom and dad plus a play zone for kids. 707 Portway Ave. (541) 321-0490 • www.pfriembeer.com

Pioneer Pizza: crusts made with organic flour. 216 E. Jewett Blvd., White Salmon (509) 493-0028 • www.pizzawhitesalmon.com

Sixth Street Bistro & Loft: Serves mostly local and organic/ sustainable food, from the free range chicken to the tasty pear salad. 509 6th St., Hood River • (541) 386-5737 • www.sixthstreetbistro.com

Sushi Okalani: A favorite, especially for the Tekka (tuna) rolls and seaweed salad. Go early before the crowds. 109 1st St., Hood River (541) 386-7423 • www.sushiokalani.com

Thai House: Delicious curries and noodles and they have a gluten free menu plus they love kids. 1302 13th St.
(541) 436-0509 • www.thaihousehoodriver.net

Trillium Café: Western style restaurant has an area filled with kid's toys and board games. 207 Oak St., Hood River • (541) 386-1996

Food To Go

Farm Stand in the Gorge: Organic and specialty foods market and deli with smoothies and locally brewed kombucha on tap, take out or eat in.
1009 12th St., Hood River • (541) 386-4203 • www.farmstandgorge.com

Feast Market and Delicatessen: Owners have two small children and want to teach them and their customers to know where their food comes from. Delicious food comes in and out their door.
320 E. Jewett Blvd., White Salmon • (509) 637-2530 • www.feastmarket.org

Lampoei's: This Thai food stand is one of our GoTos. Food is made fresh, so be prepared to wait. Located at the Windance parking lot in Hood River. Closed in the winter.

Marley's Corner Pub & Drive Thru: Grab a pastie or fish 'n chips.
1216 C St., Hood River • (541) 386-0153 • www.marleyscorner.com

Mother's Marketplace: Besides their lovely name, they sell organic produce, soups, sandwiches, pizza and smoothies to eat in the store or take out. A vegan store, no dairy or meat. 104 Hwy. 35, Hood River • (541) 387-2202

Knead: We love their pretzel bread and beware of their pastries - they're way too good! 102 5th St., Hood River • (541) 386-2048 • www.kneadhoodriver.com

North Shore Cafe: Sue loves to come here after a hard bike ride up Hospital Hill. Nutritious high quality food, fresh juices, and gluten free options. 166 E. Jewett, White Salmon
(509) 426-5341 • www.northshorecafe.weebly.com

Pine Street Bakery: Maya's favorite for the delicious scones and signature cinnamon rolls. Don't forget the baguette!
(541) 386-1719 • www.pinestreetbakery.com

Outdoor Seating

Best Western Hood River Inn: Consider Sunday brunch on their deck overlooking the river. 1108 East Marina Way, Hood River
(541) 386-2200 • www.hoodriverinn.com

Divots Clubhouse: While waiting for food and gazing at Mt. Hood, kids can putter away on the golf course. 3605 Brookside Dr., Hood River
(541) 386-7770 • www.indiancreekgolf.com

Everybody's Brewery: Fun Kids menu with tasty mac & cheese, awesome outdoor deck with a stellar view of Mt. Hood.
151 E Jewett Blvd, White Salmon, WA
(509) 637-2774 • www.everybodysbrewing.com

Hood River Taqueria: Kai's favorite, especially for the horchata and the enchiladas. 1210 13th St., Hood River
(541) 387-3300 • www.hoodrivertaqueria.com

Kickstand Coffee and Kitchen: Serves globally inspired breakfast and lunch options including housemade doughnuts and seasonal salads. Nothing wrong with kale and doughnuts. 1235 State St., Hood River
(541) 436-0016 • www.kickstandcoffee.net

RiverTap: Specials like 50 cent wings. 703 E. 2nd St., The Dalles
(541) 296-7870 • www.rivertap.com

Solera Brewery: Formerly a historic theatre, this pub serves comfort food, like hamburgers and paninis. Weather permitting, sit outside and enjoy the spectacular view. 4945 Baseline Dr., Parkdale (541) 352-5500 • www.solerabrewery.com

Solstice Wood Fire Cafe: Maya's favorite, but it can be busy. Creative pizza combinations like cherries, chorizo and goat cheese, kids love the wood-fired s'mores. The key lime pie will make your heart skip a beat. Conveniently located right across from the Waterfront playground. 501 Portway Avenue, Hood River (541) 436-0800 • www.solsticewoodfirecafe.com

Stonehedge Gardens & Bistro: During the summer, families dine outside in their garden patio. Ruth dreams about their signature mushroom ravioli with pears and onions. 3405 Wine Country Ave., Hood River (541) 386-3940 • www.stonehedgegardens.com

Three Rivers Grill: A premier view from their deck where kids can draw on the tables inside or play across the street at the library. 601 Oak St. (541) 386-8883 • www.3riversgrill.com

Walking Man's Brewery: Gourmet pub food, like grilled fish tacos, artisan pizzas and free range beef burgers. 240 SW First St., Stevenson (509) 427-5520 • walkingmanbeer.com

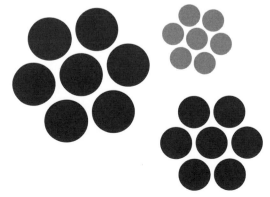

Playground and Arcade Restaurants

Andrew's Pizza & Bakery: Thin crust pizza, baked goods and a playroom. Consider pizza and a movie at their Skylight Theater.

107 Oak St., Hood River
(541) 386-1448

310 S.W. Second St., Stevenson
(509) 427-8008 • www.skylighttheatre.com

Pietro's Pizza: This popular family-eating pizza place has lots of space and a huge game room geared for older kids. 107 2nd St., Hood River
(541) 386-1606 • www.pietrosrestaurant.com

Ranch Drive-In: Popular with toddlers because half of the dining area is a playroom full of toys. The economic diner serves mainly hamburgers, french fries and shakes. Warning: you may have to wrestle your kids out of the playroom to get them to eat. 1950 12th St., Hood River • (541) 386-1155

Spooky's Pizza: Families love their pizza and games.
3320 W. 6th St., The Dalles
(541) 298-1300 • www.spookyspizza.com

Quick Bites

Boda's Kitchen: Ruth's favorite for a quick lunch from their gourmet delicatessen. 404 Oak St., Hood River • bodaskitchen.com

El Rinconcito Express: Tim says they have the best burritos around and Lisa loves their tamales.

Two places: a trailer in Hood River, 1833 Cascade Ave.
(541) 386-2911.

A bigger place in Bingen, 114 W. Steuben St.
(509) 493-8227 • www.elrinconcitoexpress.com

El Rio Burrito Bar: Fast Mexican food in downtown Hood River. The kid's menu includes tacos and burritos. 112 Oak St., Hood River
(541) 436-0099 • www.elrioburrito.com

Freshies Bagel and Juice: This high gluten zone bakes great tasting bagels that are especially delicious when hot out the oven. 13 Oak St., Hood River
(541) 386-2123

La Casa de Sabor: Quick Mexican food, perfect for take-out.
230 1st St., Stevenson • (509) 427-5423

Mi Lindo Jalisco: Taco truck in Nobi's parking lot. Lisa loves their tacos adobada. 1380 Tucker Rd., Hood River

New York City Sub Shop: Large sub sandwiches, and special one-of-a-kind peppers. 1020 Wasco St., Hood River
(541) 386-5144 • www.newyorksubshop.com

CHAPTER 18

NEED A PLACE

to Stay?

Photo by Jeff Greenwood

Rent me on www.airbnb.com!

Need a roof or tent over your head? This list will get you tucked in for a fun kid adventure. Remember the chocolate and graham crackers for s'mores. Most hotels these days are kid-friendly, but to simplify your hotel search, we just listed the ones with swimming pools.

Campgrounds—Oregon

Ainsworth State Park: Access to great hiking in waterfall alley. Exit 35 off of I-84 westbound. (800) 452-5687 • www.oregonstateparks.org

Eagle Creek Campground: Oldest forest service campground in the country. Open mid April to early October. Buck Pt. Trail #439 (541) 308-1700 • www.fs.usda.gov

Deschutes River State Rec. Area: Big grassy area, with biking and swimming. (800)-452-5687 • www.oregonstateparks.org

KOA Campground: Swimming pool. 8415 NE Forest Lane, Cascade Locks (541) 374-8668 • www.koa.com

Lost Lake Resort: Camping, fishing, swimming and more. Open May-October. (541) 386-6366 • www.lostlakeresort.org

Marine Park Campground: Especially popular with sailors. 355 WaNaPa St., Cascade Locks • (541) 374-8619 • www.portofcascadelocks.net

Memaloose: Exit 73, 11 miles east of Hood River in Mosier. (800)-452-5687 • www.oregonstateparks.org

Mt. Hood National Forest: For backpacking/camping at Vista Ridge, Tilly Jane or Cloud Cap. (503) 668-1700 • www.fs.fed.us

Tollbridge Park: 17 miles south of Hood River. (541) 352-5522 • www.co.hood-river.or.us

Tucker Park: 5 miles south of Hood River on Dee Hwy., access to the cold river. 541-386-4477 • www.co.hood-river.or.us

Viento State Park: Exit 56 off of I-84, 8 miles west of Hood River, popular with windsurfers. (800) 452-5687 • www.oregonstateparks.org

Campgrounds—Washington

Beacon Rock State Park: Great hiking to the Pool of Winds. (509) 427-8265 • www.parks.wa.gov

Columbia Hills State Park (Horsethief): Home of She Who Watches, trail where Lisa and Ruth met, fishing, grassy area. (509) 767-1159 • www.parks.wa.gov

Gifford Pinchot National Forest: Trout Lake, Wind River, Mt. Adams area, including Takhlakh Lake, a prime canoeing and camping destination. (509) 395-6002 • www.fs.fed.us/gpnf

Maryhill State Park/Peach Beach: Popular with the windsurfing crowd, right on the river. (509) 773-4698 • www.parks.wa.gov

Photo by Paloma Ayala • www.fotoisphoto.com

Roosevelt/Rock Creek: 17 miles east of Maryhill, no fees. (541) 506-7819 • www.nwp.usace.army.mil

Timberlake Campground: Huge gathering hall, fireplace. 112 Bylin Rd., Home Valley • (509) 427-2267 www.timberlakecampgroundandrvpark.com

Vacation Rentals

Columbia Gorge Vacation Rentals: (866) 312-2312 • www.columbiagorgevacationsrentals.com

Gorge Central Vacation Rentals: (541) 386-6109 • www.gorgecentral.com

Gorge Rentals: (800) 387-4787 • www.GorgeRentals.com

VRBO.com and Airbnb: Rent directly from a home owner.

Hotels with Pools and/or Spas

Best Western Cascade Locks: 735 WaNaPa St., Cascade Locks
(541) 374-8777 • www.bwcolumbiariverinn.com

Best Western Hood River: 1108 E. Marina Way, Hood River
541-386-2200 • www.hoodriverinn.com

Bonneville Hot Springs Resort & Spa:
1252 East Cascade Dr., North Bonneville
866-459-1678 • www.bonnevilleresort.com

Columbia Gorge Riverside Lodge (outdoor soaking pool):
200 SW Cascade Ave., Stevenson
(509) 427-5650 • www.cgriversidelodge.com

Comfort Inn: 351 Lone Pine Dr., The Dalles
(541) 298-2800 • www.comfortinn.com

Hampton Inn: Scheduled to open Spring 2016. 1 Nichols Way, Hood River

Skamania Lodge: 1131 SW Skamania Lodge Way, Stevenson
800-221-7117 • www.skamania.com

Shilo Inn Suites Hotel: 3223 Bret Clodfelter Way, The Dalles
800-222-2244, www.shiloinns.com

Super 8 Motel: 609 Cherry Heights Rd., The Dalles
(541) 296-6888 • www.super8.com

The Dalles Inn: 112 W. 2nd St., The Dalles
(888) 935-2378, www.thedallesinn.com

Hotels Offering Year Round Mountain Fun

Cooper Spur Mountain Resort: 10755 Cooper Spur Rd., Mt. Hood • (541) 352-6692 • www.cooperspur.com

Timberline Lodge: 27500 W Leg Rd. (503) 272-3311 • www.timberlinelodge.com

About the Authors

Ruth Berkowitz

A writer, mediator and lawyer, Ruth loves adventure. She's been Kidding Around the Gorge since 2001 when her family moved to Hood River. At the time, there was no road map, guiding young families, so she teamed with Jody Barringer and wrote the first Kidding Around the Gorge. In 2008, Ruth and her husband followed through on their marital promise and took their kids on a three year sailing adventure. They sailed under the Golden Gate Bridge, journeyed south to Ecuador and then across the Pacific to Australia, with hundreds of stops along the way. Her advice to families is to seize the moment -- after all -- life is about the journey, not the destination.

Lisa Kosglow

An outdoor enthusiast, Lisa rides her mountain bike, shreds powder days on Mt. Hood and digs in the dirt in her organic garden. In her past life, Lisa represented the United States on the US Olympic Snowboard Team in Salt Lake City, Utah (2002) and Nagano, Japan (1998). After spending almost 20 summers in the Gorge training on Mt. Hood, she moved to Hood River full time in 2004. She and her husband, also an Olympic snowboarder, are raising their 5 year old daughter here. Lisa founded Let's Get Out Adventure Camps so she can help kids play, connect and thrive in the outdoors. Her advice to families is to pack a lot of snacks and get outside together.

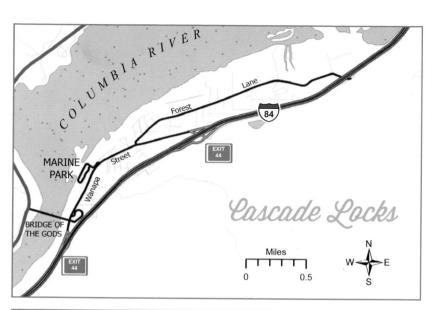

COLUMBIA RIVER

Lane

Forest

84

EXIT 44

MARINE PARK

Street

Wanapa

BRIDGE OF THE GODS

EXIT 44

Cascade Locks

Miles

0   0.5

N
W   E
S

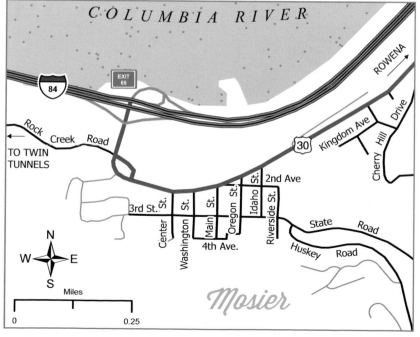

COLUMBIA RIVER

84

EXIT 69

ROWENA

Rock Creek Road

TO TWIN TUNNELS

30

Kingdom Ave

Cherry Hill Drive

2nd Ave

3rd St. St.

Center St.

Washington St.

Main St.

4th Ave.

Oregon St.

Idaho St.

Riverside St.

State Road

Huskey Road

N
W   E
S

Miles

0   0.25

Mosier

225

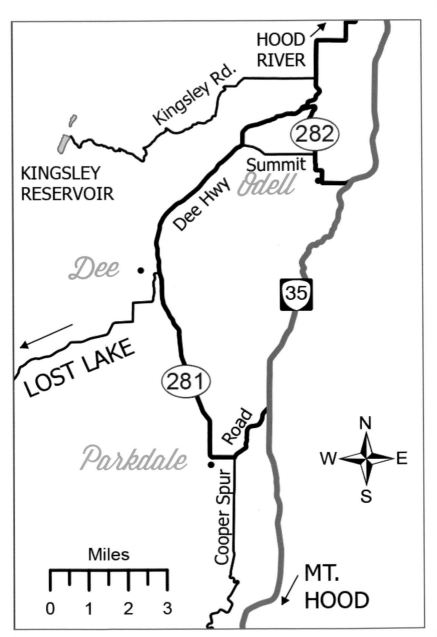

HOOD RIVER

KINGSLEY RESERVOIR

Kingsley Rd.

282

Summit

Odell

Dee

Dee Hwy

35

LOST LAKE

281

Parkdale

Road

Cooper Spur

N
W E
S

Miles

0 1 2 3

MT. HOOD

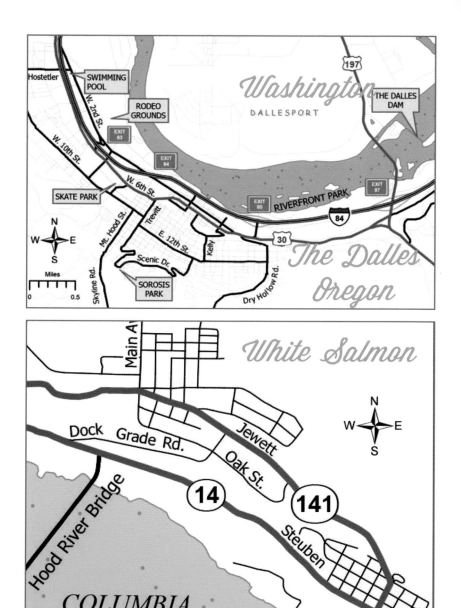

Appendix B
KIDDING AROUND BY AREA

Index

233

Notes

Email your ideas and photos to kiddingaroundthegorge@gmail.com.
Like us on Facebook www.facebook.com/kiddingaroundthegorge.

Notes